W9-BCG-254

WriteRight
An English Handbook

i

Acknowledgements

This English handbook was developed by members of the Stevens Point Area Public Schools, Stevens Point, Wisconsin. Coordinators of the publication were:

> Dennis Bonikowske
> Jean LaDue
> Harold J. Olson
> Pauline M. Phillips

The handbook was designed to be used as an aid for high school students in the Stevens Point District as part of the Competency Based Education Program.

Phi Delta Kappa wishes to express its heartiest thanks to the Stevens Point Area Public Schools for making this handbook available for nationwide dissemination. Phi Delta Kappa is also very proud to know that the handbook was developed as a result of the district's adoption of Phi Delta Kappa's Educational Planning Model. The use of the planning model led to identification of a need for sequenced instruction and improvement of instruction in English composition and usage for all students.

Wilmer K. Bugher, Associate Executive Secretary for Administration, wishes to express his appreciation for the opportunity to select the handbook for nationwide dissemination. Phi Delta Kappa acknowledges and expresses its appreciation to Carol Kelleghan for her excellent editorial work on the handbook.

Finally, it is Phi Delta Kappa's belief that the handbook, with its unique alphabetical index, will prove valuable for school, home, or office use. The handbook is available from Phi Delta Kappa's Center for Dissemination of Innovative Programs, Eighth & Union Sts., Box 789, Bloomington, IN 47402. Telephone (812)339-1156.

First published 1980
Reprinted 1980, 1981, 1984,
1985, 1986, 1987,
Reprinted with minor revisions 1988

Introduction

Although most Americans begin to practice using the English language at the time they utter their first words, many students and adults still find writing the language unnatural and complicated. As a matter of fact, if you crinkle up your nose and mumble disgustedly when someone mentions "English" or "grammar," your reactions probably match those of a majority of students in high schools throughout the country. Nevertheless, although we are often unwilling to admit it, we usually admire those people who use our language well: those who can vividly recreate an experience in a letter or a story, those who can write a clear, orderly explanation of a program or project, and those who can persuade us to do something with convincing, forceful argument.

Writing and good English usage are not easy for many of us. Avoiding common errors in speaking and writing is no simple task, but neither is it an impossible assignment. Writing and good English usage are skills and, like most other skills, they can be improved with study and practice. It may seem difficult and awkward at first, but with practice, not just in English classes but in all situations that require written efforts, writing can become much more natural. Every field of study has its technical language, the words, phrases, and symbols that explain how something works. That's what grammar does; it explains how the language works and therefore gives you a fuller understanding and greater command of the language.

This book is not an English textbook, but a handbook, listing in alphabetical order the most common terms and techniques necessary to write our language. It can serve as a student handbook, as a home-study reference, or as a reference for office use. It is detailed enough to solve most or all of the everyday problems that come up in writing or special composition.

The handbook is organized into three sections:

Part I: Alphabetical Reference Section
Part II: Principles of Writing
Part III: Special Composition Forms

In addition to being used as quick reference, Part II may be read independently as an introduction to the principles of writing before beginning a composition, or may actually be used in conjunction with classroom instruction.

It is important for the reader to note that several of the sections in the handbook deal with style rules that are a matter of convention and may vary in situations where other equally viable style rules have been adopted.

It is Phi Delta Kappa's hope that this booklet will meet the growing need of writers to be able to quickly find answers to their questions concerning the English language. Any suggestions for improvement or correction would be greatly appreciated and should be mailed to Dr. Neville Robertson, Phi Delta Kappa, Box 789, Bloomington, IN 47402.

84315

Part I: Alphabetical Reference Section

Abbreviations. As a general principle abbreviations should not be used in formal writing. Exceptions include footnotes and some types of technical writing where abbreviations of lengthy technical terminology are more easily recognized than the terms themselves. Special instances in which abbreviations are used include:

1. Mr., Mrs., Ms., Messrs., Mmes., Dr., Rev., when used as titles before names; Jr., Sr., and college degrees A.B., B.S., and Ph.D., when used after a name.

   Note: In formal writing, titles such as Reverend, Honorable, President, Professor, and Senator are not abbreviated.

2. Indications of time, A.D., B.C., A.M., P.M., when used with figures.

   Examples: A.D. 275
   9:17 A.M.
   12:23 P.M.
   315 B.C.

3. Formal Latin expressions such as:

etc.	...for...	et cetera	...meaning...	and so forth
e.g.		exempli gratia		for example
i.e.		id est		that is
et. al.		et alli		and others

4. Generally understood abbreviations of government agencies: FBI, FAA, FDIC, IRS.

5. Zip code abbreviations of state names.

Punctuation of Abbreviations. Periods are used after abbreviations except for names of government agencies referred to by their initials or technical abbreviations which serve as symbols: Na, H_2O, cos, tan.

Note: An abbreviation coming at the end of the sentence is punctuated by the period ending the sentence.

Example: Tom will be here at 10:30 A.M.

2

Zip Code Abbreviations of State Names.

State	Abbrev.	State	Abbrev.
Alabama	AL	Montana	MT
Alaska	AK	Nebraska	NE
Arizona	AZ	Nevada	NV
Arkansas	AR	New Hampshire	NH
California	CA	New Jersey	NJ
Colorado	CO	New Mexico	NM
Connecticut	CT	New York	NY
Delaware	DE	North Carolina	NC
District of Columbia	DC	North Dakota	ND
Florida	FL	Ohio	OH
Georgia	GA	Oklahoma	OK
Hawaii	HI	Oregon	OR
Idaho	ID	Pennsylvania	PA
Illinois	IL	Puerto Rico	PR
Indiana	IN	Rhode Island	RI
Iowa	IA	South Carolina	SC
Kansas	KS	South Dakota	SD
Kentucky	KY	Tennessee	TN
Louisiana	LA	Texas	TX
Maine	ME	Utah	UT
Maryland	MD	Vermont	VT
Massachusetts	MA	Virginia	VA
Michigan	MI	Washington	WA
Minnesota	MN	West Virginia	WV
Mississippi	MS	Wisconsin	WI
Missouri	MO	Wyoming	WY

Adjective. Adjectives are words, phrases, or clauses used to modify (describe) nouns or pronouns. Adjectives often answer the questions: Which one? What kind? How many? How much?

Adjective	Noun	Tells
that	football	(which game)
old	uniforms	(what kind)
ten	players	(how many)
several	errors	(how much)

Adjectives fill certain positions in a sentence. They regularly occur between a determiner and a noun in both the complete subject and the complete predicate of a sentence. They also serve as predicate complements following a linking verb.

Some adjectives are marked by endings (suffixes). Some recognizable adjective endings are:

able	The *changeable* weather kept us home.
y	The *rusty* windmill made a weird noise.
less	The *helpless* child cried for his mother.
ful	Three *colorful* movies were shown.
ible	The *invisible* man showed up.
ive	It was a *festive* dinner.

Adjectives are sometimes marked by signal words (intensifiers) including: *very, quite, too, rather, somewhat, more, most.*

Adjectives, Comparative, and Superlative Degree. Most adjectives form their degree by adding *er*. The comparative degree is used when *two* objects are compared.

Example: Of the *two* schools, ours is the *larger*.

The superlative degree is formed by adding *est*. The superlative degree is used when *more than two* objects are compared.

Example: Of the *three* schools, ours is the *largest*.

Adjective	Comparative	Superlative
tall	taller	tallest
old	older	oldest
fine	finer	finest
shiny	shinier	shiniest
easy	easier	easiest

If an adjective has more than two syllables, *more, most, less,* or *least* must be added before it instead of *er* or *est*.

beautiful	*more* beautiful	*most* beautiful
successful	*less* successful	*least* successful

Some two-syllable adjectives must also have *more, most, less,* or *least,* so always check a dictionary to be sure when to use them.

likely	*more* likely	*most* likely

Some adjectives make their comparative and superlative degree by complete word changes. Here are two important ones to remember:

good	better	best
bad	worse	worst

4

Adverb. Adverbs are words, phrases, or clauses used to modify a verb, adjective, or another adverb. Most adverbs modify verbs.

An adverb often answers the questions: How? When? Where? or To what extent? (How often? or How much?) the action of the verb is done.

He ate *enthusiastically*.	(how)
The paper arrived *late*.	(when)
He sang *there*.	(where)
The speaker droned on *forever*.	(to what extent)
Please, *never* eat rabbit in my house.	(to what extent)

Adverbs often end in *ly* because *ly* added to an adjective makes an adverb.

Example: Adjective describes *what*: The girl is *calm*.
Adverb describes *how*: She *calmly* pushed him into the pool.

The following words are always adverbs: *not, never,* and *very.*

Some nouns may be used as adverbs.

Examples: I called her *yesterday*.
We expect them *Sunday*.
They are leaving *tomorrow*.

Signal words (intensifiers) including *very, rather, quite,* and many others often mark adverbs within a sentence. Adverbs often occur at the end of a sentence, but they are more movable than other form classes.

Adverbs, Comparative, and Superlative Degree. Most adverbs which end in *ly* form their comparative degree with the word *more* and their superlative degree with the word *most.*

Adverb	Comparative	Superlative
quickly	*more* quickly	*most* quickly
dreamily	*more* dreamily	*most* dreamily

Some adverbs add *er* for the comparative and *est* for the superlative:

soon	sooner	soonest
fast	faster	fastest

Some adverbs make their comparative and superlative degree by complete word changes:

well	better	best
much	more	most
little	less	least

To determine whether or not a word is an adverb, check the word to see if it properly completes either of the following sentences:

He said it _____.

He _____ said it.

Intensifiers. Adverbs such as *very, much,* and *too* sometimes intensify (strengthen) meaning; they are therefore called intensifiers. They are often used to introduce adjectives. The superlative of adjectives and adverbs also may be classed as intensifiers.

Antonyms. A word which is opposite in meaning to that of another word is an antonym: *sad* is the antonym of *happy, small* and *little* are antonyms of *large.* Just as there are no exact synonyms, antonyms are not precisely opposite either. See *Synonyms.*

Apostrophe ('). An apostrophe is used:

1. To show possession. See *Possessives.*

2. To take the place of the omitted letter or letters in a contraction. See *Contractions.*

3. To form plurals of letters, figures, and words referred to as words:

    He confuses *u's* and *n's* and has left out the *and's.*

Appositive. An appositive is a noun or pronoun that directly follows another noun or pronoun to rename, explain, or identify it.

Example: My *sister Mary* ate the pie. *Mary* renames and identifies *sister* so it is an appositive.

Appositives that contain more than one word are called appositive phrases and are set off by commas.

Example: The *girl, a student at SPASH,* plays football. *A student at SPASH* is an appositive phrase, identifying the *girl.*

6

Brackets [ ]. An explanation, comment, or correction that has been inserted into quoted material is often set off by brackets. This implies that the inserted material is put in by the person writing the quote, not the person quoted.

Example: According to critic Lucille Leahy:
"Without a doubt Jane Austen's study of a nineteenth century English county town [*Pride and Prejudice*] is a masterpiece of quiet comedy."

Brackets are also used as parentheses within parentheses.

Example: The population is over 24,000 (See Appendix B [Chart IV] on page 21).

Capital Letters. Capital letters are used for the following:

1. First word of every sentence.

2. First word, last word, and all important words in titles.

3. First word in the complimentary close of a letter.

4. Important words in the salutation of a letter.

5. First word of a direct quotation.

6. In outlining, the first word of each main idea and subhead.

7. Names of buildings, monuments, and parks.

8. Names of churches and religious denominations (*First Methodist, Catholic*).

9. Names of countries, languages, races, nationalities, and political parties.

10. Names of the days of the week, the months of the year, and special days (holidays).

11. Names of firms (*American Potato, Sentry Insurance*) and organizations (*Boy Scouts of America*).

12. Names of persons.

13. Names of rivers, oceans, seas, lakes, bays, gulfs, and mountains.

14. Names of schools.

15. Names of states.

16. Names of streets.

17. Names of towns and cities.

18. The word *I*.

19. The titles of people if the title precedes the person's name (*Lord Byron, President Lincoln*).

20. *The Bible* and its books and words referring to *God*.

21. Initials (*F. D. Roosevelt*) and abbreviations for time (*A.D., P.M.*).

22. Copyrighted names, brand names, and trademarks (*Jello, Spearmint gum, Kleenex tissue, Volkswagon Rabbit*). Note that the noun that follows a brand name is not capitalized unless it is part of the brand name.

23. Historical events, periods, and documents (*the Industrial Revolution, the Middle Ages, the Declaration of Independence*).

24. Names of fields of study which are derived from proper nouns or the names of languages; others are not capitalized unless they are specific course titles (*German, Early European History, Algebra I*).

25. Proper nouns or adjectives formed from proper nouns within names of animals, birds, flowers, trees, diseases, games, foods, and seasons, but not the words they modify (*Easter lily, German shepherd, white bass, white pine, white Dutch clover, whiteface Hereford, whitetail deer, praying mantis, spoonbill, mayfly, meadowlark*).

26. Names of geographical regions (*the Midwest*) but not points of the compass (*walk west five miles*).

27. Mother, father, sister, aunt, and so on only when they are used as part of a person's name (*Aunt Sue*) or as a substitute for the person's name (*ask Mom for the car*).

When in doubt, check a recent dictionary.

Clauses. A clause is a group of words containing both a subject and a verb and used as a part of a sentence. Clauses may be categorized according to completeness of the thought expressed as either *independent clauses* or *subordinate clauses*.

Independent Clause. The independent clause (also called main clause) when removed from its sentence could stand alone as a sentence, for it expresses a complete thought in itself. In the following sentences the independent clauses are italicized and the subject and verb identified:

      S V   S V
Tom is late, but *he can still finish the project.*

                       S V   V
Although Terry sings well, *she may not join the choir.*

Subordinate Clause. The subordinate clause (also called dependent clause) cannot stand alone as a sentence, for it must depend on an independent clause to complete the thought expressed. In the following sentences the subordinate clauses are italicized and the subject and verb identified:

S   V
When I complete this work, I am going home.

S V
The coat *that I like* is available only in blue.

The subordinate clause cannot stand alone, and is always used within a sentence just as a single word is used: as an adjective, or an adverb, or a noun.

Adjective Clause. The adjective clause is a subordinate clause that modifies a noun or a pronoun. It is usually introduced by a pronoun (*who, whose, whom, which, that*) called a *relative pronoun* because it relates back to the noun or pronoun being modified by the clause.

Note: The relative pronoun introducing the adjective clause usually functions not only as the link between the clause and the word modified by the clause but also as a subject or object within the clause itself.

Examples:

Jerry is the boy *who helped me.*	The relative pronoun *who* introduces the subordinate clause and acts as its *subject.*
The boy *whom he liked* was always helpful.	The relative pronoun *whom* introduces the subordinate clause and acts as the *direct object* of the clause.

Adverb Clause. The adverb clause is a subordinate clause that modifies a verb, adjective, or adverb. It is usually introduced by a conjunction, called a *subordinating conjunction*, which links the clause to the rest of the sentence and answers one of the questions How? When? Where? or How much?

SC S V

Examples: *After we left the game*, Tom went home.

SC S   V
I slept *while they did the dishes.*

Note: 1. Common subordinating conjunctions include:

after	if	when
although	since	where
as	than	whether
as if	unless	while
because	until	
before		

2. An adverb clause coming at the beginning of a sentence is set off by a comma.

Noun Clause. The noun clause is a subordinate clause used as a noun. The noun clause usually begins with a subordinate conjunction (*if, since, because*) or a relative pronoun (*who, whom, which*) and may be found anywhere in a sentence where a single word noun might be used. A noun clause may be the subject, direct object, predicate complement, indirect object, object of preposition, or an appositive.

Examples: Subject: *What he says* is important.
Direct Object: Give me *whatever is left.*
Predicate Complement: We are *what we eat.*

Cliche´or Trite Expressions. A trite expression (or cliché) is a phrase that is worn out by use. It may be an expression that has been around for many years, such as *take a dim view, the worse for wear, dyed in the wool*; or it may be a more current expression that has caught on too quickly and too well, such as *do your own thing, play it cool,* or *right on.* This doesn't mean that such expressions are never to be used. It is best, however, not to use them too often. If overused, cliché´s like the ones listed here, cause writing to lack freshness, individuality, sincerity, and suspense.

Father Time	fresh as a daisy
Mother Nature	common faults
darkness overtook us	tried and true
prime of life	roared down the street
as fate would have it	roared like a lion
crack of dawn	cried like a baby
flowing with milk and honey	bolt of lightning
bolt from the blue	dark and dreary day
ran like a flash	tear-stained face
quick as a wink	heartfelt sympathy
staff of life	weeping girl
honest work	all of a sudden
thread of life	gorgeous sunset
to burn the midnight oil	eyed suspiciously
broad daylight	popped the question
ghostly fog	filled to overflowing
smooth as silk	old soldiers never die

sharp as a knife	better late than never
razor sharp	a good time was had by all
hair's breadth	breathed a sigh of relief
teetered on the brink	sticks out like a sore thumb
like peaches and cream	no time like the present
beady-eyed	last but not least
smooth curve	undying love
wise move	hopeless task
blinding light	early dawn
black as coal	arms of love
white as snow	feeling great
gnarled oak	topsy-turvy
mile a minute	blind as a bat
crisp, cool	free as a bird
by hook or crook	

Colon (:). The colon is a rather formal and emphatic mark that directs attention to what follows. It has four main uses:

1. A colon is used to introduce a list of appositives (at the end of a sentence) that the writer wants to emphasize.

    Example: Lee recommended her three favorite novels: *Catch—22, Go Tell It on the Mountain,* and *Great Expectations.*

    A colon usually is not used directly after a verb:

    Example: Her favorite novels are *Catch—22, Go Tell It on the Mountain,* and *Great Expectations.*

2. A colon is used to introduce a long or formal quotation in factual writing.

    Example: Malcolm Crowley wrote of F. Scott Fitzgerald and the Jazz Age:

    > Fitzgerald not only represented the age but came to suspect that he had helped to create it, by setting forth a pattern of conduct that would be followed by persons a little younger than himself. That it was a dangerous pattern was something he recognized almost from the beginning.

3. A colon is used after a statement which is followed by an explanation:

    > White didn't care that the program failed: none of his money was involved.

    > Jane never went back to Eagle River: her experiences there had been too painful.

    > Trying to please the manager was useless: she was critical of everything we did.

4. The colon has several additional uses:

    A. After the salutation in a business letter.
        Dear Mr. Sutton: Gentlemen:

    B. Between hours and minutes expressed in figures.
        9:35 A.M.   8:15 P.M.

    C. Between volume and page numbers of a magazine.
        National Geographic, 113:795-837

    D. Between Biblical chapter and verse.
        Matthew 2:5   II Corinthians 5:1-3

    E. Separating title and subtitle of a book.
        The Crisis: Energy in the Eighties

In typing, the colon is followed by two spaces before the next word.

Comma (,). A comma is used:

1. Between the name of a town and the name of the state and after the state unless the name of the state ends the sentence.

    Example: We moved from Miami, Florida, to Stevens Point, Wisconsin.

2. Between the day of the month and the year and after the year unless it is the end of the sentence.

    Example: On June 22, 1965, I entered school.

3. Between the words or groups of words in a series, including before the words *and* or *or*.

    Example: Joe, Bill, and Pete are my dragons.

4. To set off the name words in direct address.

    Example: Jane, bring me your answers.

5. To separate a direct quotation from the rest of the sentence.

    Example: "I'll referee the game," he said.

6. After a word like oh, well, gosh, phew, yes, no, etc.

    Example: Well, I'll leave now.

7. To set off appositives.

    Example: The Fox, an old theater, is on Main Street.

8. To set off elements which are not important to the basic meaning of the sentence, usually subordinate clauses.

    Example: Arthur, who dislikes work, is failing chemistry.

9. After introductory clauses and verbal phrases.

    Example: Since you are an experienced skier, suppose you demonstrate the slalom.

    Watching the hockey players, Stash began to wish he could skate.

Complement. A complement is a word or expression used to complete an idea indicated or implied by a verb.

Objective Complement. The objective complement helps to complete the meaning of some action verbs. It may be a noun or an adjective and usually follows the direct object. If a noun, it tells what the direct object is named, elected, or made to be.

Example: They elected Jean chairman.

The noun *chairman* refers to the direct object *Jean* and helps to complete the meaning of the verb *elected.* It is an objective complement.

Example: The students made her angry.

The adjective *angry* modifies the direct object *her* and helps to complete the meaning of the verb *made.* It is an objective complement.

Predicate Complement. The predicate complement is a noun, pronoun, or adjective which comes after a linking verb and describes or identifies the subject. See also *Predicate Adjective* and *Predicate Noun.*

Conjunctions. Conjunctions are connecting words used to join single words, phrases, clauses, and even sentences. Conjunctions may be grouped into two categories according to the relationship they establish between the words, phrases, or clauses they join.

Coordinating Conjunction. Coordinating conjunctions, including *and, but, or, nor,* and *for,* are used to join single words to single words (Tom *and* Joe); phrases to phrases (across the yard *and* up the steps); and clauses to clauses (Where are you going, *and* what are you doing?). Coordinating conjunctions used in this manner indicate that the ideas as well as the grammatical forms being joined are of equal value.

Subordinating Conjunction. Subordinating conjunctions, including such words as *although, after, if, since,* and *because,* are used to connect subordinate clauses to independent clauses.

Example: *Although* he is short, he will be able to reach the shelf.

Subordinating conjunctions used in this manner indicate that the idea contained in the subordinate clause is less important than or dependent on the idea expressed in the main clause. See also *Adverb Clause* for a more complete list of subordinating conjunctions.

Conjunctive Adverb. Adverbs used as connectives to join short, choppy sentences into longer sentences are called conjunctive adverbs. These adverbs not only join independent clauses, but also clarify the relationships between the clauses, making writing not only smoother but clearer.

Examples: The coach was tired. The practice was cut short.

The coach was tired; *therefore,* the practice was cut short.
(*Therefore* shows that the second clause is a result of the first.)

Some common conjunctive adverbs are:

accordingly	hence	otherwise
also	however	so
anyhow	indeed	still
besides	likewise	then
consequently	moreover	therefore
furthermore	nevertheless	thus
		yet

Some of these connectives are more suitable to formal usage (See also *Usage.*) such as: *consequently, furthermore,* and *moreover.* But the simpler ones are useful ways of making your writing clearer and more forceful even in informal situations.

When used between two independent clauses as a parenthetical, a conjunctive adverb is punctuated by placing a semicolon before the adverb and comma after it. When the adverb comes within a clause, it is set off by commas.

Examples: I may go to see the film; *furthermore*, if it's good, I may see it twice.

He read the letter hurriedly; *then* he put on his gloves and left. (Because *then* is not used as a parenthetical, it is not set off with a comma.)

George left home; he was, *consequently*, nowhere to be found when they needed him.

Contractions. A contraction is a shorter way of writing two words. Use an apostrophe in a contraction at the place where letters have been omitted.

Examples: Please *don't* eat the daisies.

Music's the medicine of a troubled mind.

Contractions are not generally acceptable in formal writing and are out of place in standard English except when used to convey the actual tone and flavor of dialogue.

Some examples of contractions are:

are not	*aren't*	I am	*I'm*	they have	*they've*
can not	*can't*	I have	*I've*	was not	*wasn't*
do not	*don't*	is not	*isn't*	we are	*we're*
does not	*doesn't*	it is	*it's*	we have	*we've*
had not	*hadn't*	of the clock	*o'clock*	were not	*weren't*
has not	*hasn't*	should not	*shouldn't*	who is	*who's*
have not	*haven't*	there is	*there's*	would not	*wouldn't*
he is	*he's*	they are	*they're*	will not	*won't*
how is	*how's*				

Dash (—). The dash is a mark of punctuation most characteristically used to denote a sudden break or shift in thought. A dash is nearly equivalent to a comma (both may be used in pairs or alone, and between expressions of coordinate or unequal rank). The dash is useful to convey a special emphasis or contrast, but, if too frequently used it reveals ignorance of the correct use of other marks of punctuation and makes for a choppy, incoherent style.

The dash is the only common mark of punctuation not on the standard typewriter keyboard. To type a dash, use two hyphens; no space precedes or follows the hyphens. Only in typing is the dash equal to two hyphens; the printed hyphen is smaller than half a dash. Use a dash:

1. To indicate a break or shift in thought.

Example: Ann Farland — she used to be our baby-sitter — is graduating from law school this spring.

2. To show a sudden interruption or hesitation, especially in dialogue, a dash can be used effectively.

Example: "As soon as the game starts, our team — here they come — here they are now."

"You mean —," Joe began.

"I — I — I didn't take your bracelet!"

3. After a list of items or names and before the summarizing words *all* or *all these*.

Example: Joe, Sam, Lefty, Slugger, and Tom — all the old gang was together again.

4. To mean "namely" or "in other words" before an explanation at the end of a sentence.

Example: There was only one person I didn't want along on our trip — my brother.

Direct Object. A direct object is a noun or pronoun that follows an action verb like *hit, bake, kick, throw, sing.*

DO
Examples: John hit the *wall.*

DO
Mother baked a *cake.*

DO
Don't kick the *dog.*

The direct object receives the action of the verb or shows the results of the action. To find the direct object, first find the action verb and then ask the question "What or whom?" The noun that answers the question is the direct object.

DO
Example: Mother baked a *cake.* Ask — "Mother baked what?" Answer — "a *cake.*" *Cake* is the direct object.

Division of Words. It is sometimes necessary to divide words at the ends of lines in order to keep a fairly straight right-hand margin on a formal paper. Whenever this occurs, break the word between syllables. Words should be divided according to the following rules:

1. Both parts should be pronounceable; words of one syllable should not be divided.

   Examples: *through, drained, you're, stayed*

2. A single letter should not stand by itself.

   Examples: *alone* or *scratchy* should not be divided

3. Generally, divide a word before a suffix or after a prefix.

   Examples: *re-arrange, thought-less, non-violent*

4. Generally, divide between double consonants.

   Examples: *rac-coon, stop-ping, gram-mar*

   Note: If the double consonants come at the end of the root word, they are not split; divide after the double consonants, before such endings as *ing, er,* and *able.*

   Examples: *call-ing, putt-er, spill-able*

5. Divide consonants that come between two vowels if they are pronounced separately.

   Examples: *stil-ted, fes-ter, sig-nal*

6. Two vowels pronounced separately may be divided.

   Examples: *ge-ography, cre-ation, ide-alize*

7. Do not divide two consonants or two vowels that are pronounced as one sound.

   Examples: *sock-et, clea-ver, poi-son*

8. Generally, divide between the parts of a compound word.

   Examples: *man-hole, down-trodden, feed-lot*

9. If the word is normally spelled with a hyphen, divide at the hyphen.

   Examples: *garden-variety, round-shouldered, poverty-stricken*

10. If a single consonant comes between two voiced vowels, the consonant usually begins the syllable with the second vowel.

    Examples: *se-dan, imi-tation, ra-dio*

But if the preceding vowel is short and accented, keep the consonant with that vowel.

Examples: *ped-estrian, hov-el, tol-erant*

11. Avoid dividing words if readers will be confused about the meaning or pronunciation.

Not:	hide-ous	But:	hid-eous
	miser-able		mis-erable

Double Negatives. A double negative occurs in a sentence that uses two negative terms when only one is needed.

Examples:	incorrect:	She didn't say nothing to him.
	correct:	She didn't say anything to him.
	or	
	correct:	She said nothing to him.
	incorrect:	You shouldn't never do that to a dog.
	correct:	You shouldn't ever do that to a dog.
	or	
	correct:	You should never do that to a dog.
	incorrect:	Tom is scarcely never early.
	correct:	Tom is scarcely ever early.
	incorrect:	That don't make no difference.
	correct:	That doesn't make any difference.

Don't use a negative verb with *hardly, scarcely, neither, only,* or *but* (when it means *only*).

incorrect:	They don't hardly do any work.
correct:	They do hardly any work.
incorrect:	I won't scarcely have time.
correct:	I'll scarcely have time.
incorrect:	Hardly no people live here.
correct:	Hardly any people live here.
incorrect:	I don't believe in it neither.
correct:	I don't believe in it either.

Ellipsis (. . .). An ellipsis is the omission from a sentence of a word or words which would fulfill or strengthen meaning. To show such omission ellipsis periods (. . .) are normally used. Ellipsis is commonly used:

1. To indicate that words have been omitted within a quoted passage.

    Example: ". . . nothing walks with aimless feet."
    Tennyson

2. To indicate halting speech or an unfinished sentence in dialogue.

    Example: "I'm really . . . I mean . . . like . . . sorry," he faltered and fell silent.

Exclamation Point (!). An exclamation point is used at the end of sentences that express strong emotions. Too frequent use weakens its effectiveness.

Example: "Hit it!" the water skier cried.

Expletive. An expletive is a word or phrase added either to fill out a sentence or to provide emphasis. The words *it* and *there* are called expletives when they begin sentences in which the subject of the sentence follows the verb.

       Ex V   S
Example: *There* are three boxes sitting on the table.

Beginning a sentence with *it* or *there* should be avoided, for they delay the subject of the sentence into the predicate, and also require weak linking verbs (is, are) which weaken the impact of the sentence.

Heteronyms. Two or more words that have identical spelling but different meanings and pronunciations are called heteronyms.

Example: bass (the musical tone, pronounced "base")
              bass (the fish, rhyming with "pass").

Homonyms. Words that have the same pronunciation but differ in meaning are called homonyms.

Examples: male — mail, read — red, pray — prey

The meaning of such words is usually made clear by the context, but their spelling is likely to cause trouble. These may help you remember:

minister goes to the altar	tailor alters a suit
ship's bow	tree's bough
the Capitol building	capital of Wisconsin
sincere compliment	predicate complement
apple's core	Marine Corps
council meeting	defense counsel
box of stationery	a stationary windmill

Hyphen (-). The hyphen is more a mark of spelling than of punctuation. A hyphen is appropriate in the following situations:

1. With compound modifiers. Two or more words used as a single adjective preceding a noun are generally hyphenated:

   a matter-of-fact attitude   A well-timed entrance

   If the compound modifier comes after the noun, or if the first part is an adverb ending in *ly*, no hyphen is used:

   Example: Her entrance was well timed.
   An unusually short man wearing a badly tailored suit sat beside me.

   Compound proper adjectives or compound proper nouns used as adjectives are not hyphenated:

old English sheepdog	Fifth Avenue fashions
South African product	New England highway

2. With compound numbers from *twenty-one* to *ninety-nine* and fractions used as modifiers.

   one-half cup   one hundred twenty-nine

3. With prefixes. A hyphen is used between a prefix and a proper noun or adjective.

anti-Communist	pre-Victorian
ex-President Hoover	pro-British

   When a prefix ends in a vowel and a root word begins with the same vowel, a hyphen is used to prevent pronouncing the two vowels as one sound:

re-elected	anti-imperialistic
pre-eminent	

Cooperate and *coordinate*, which begin with *co* are often written as a solid word.

A hyphen is used to avoid confusion with another word that has the same spelling but a different pronunciation and meaning:

Example: They stayed at a *resort.*
I had to *re-sort* the cards.

A hyphen is used after the prefixes *self* and *ex* when *ex* means "former":

self-confident	ex-member
self-conscious	ex-soldier

4. With compound words. Since there is no simple rule for hyphenating ordinary compound words because usage varies so widely, consult a dictionary to check them.

5. For dividing a word at the end of a line of writing.

Idioms. An idiom is a combination of words that seems perfectly natural to the native speakers of a language but seems odd or peculiar to other people (usually because it has a meaning different from the literal meaning of the words).

catch a cold	make the fur fly
dip into a book	walk on air
strike a bargain	be on pins and needles
run across an old friend	take after one's father/mother

In English, the most common difficulties with idioms arise from the fact that many words idiomatically require a particular preposition to complete their meaning. Below is a partial list of these prepositional idioms:

accommodate oneself *to* a situation	coincides *with*
accommodate someone else *with* a favor	compare *to* (to show likeness)
	compare *with* (to show difference)
in accordance *with*	comply *with*
accuse *of*	concentrate *on* the problem
acquit *of*	concern *for* the safety
adapted *to* her surroundings	concur *in* a decision
addicted *to*	concur *with* a person
agree *with* a person	convenient *for* a purpose
agree *to* a proposal	convenient *to* a place
agree *on* a plan	corresponds *with* (the same as)
allergic *to*	critical *of* the rules
angry *with* a person	desist *from*
angry *at* a thing	devoid *of*
averse *to*, aversion *to* (or for) work	differ *with* a person
based *on* the facts	differ *from* (this differs from that)
capable *of*	differ *about* or *over* a question

different *from*
dissent *from*
envious *of* her luck
expert *in*
fascinated *by* the snake
independent *of*
inferior *to* his sister
insensible *of* feelings
monopoly *of*, monopoly *on*

oblivious *of* time
part *from* a person
part *with* a possession
plan *to*
proficient *in*
rewarded *with* an A
similar *to*
vexed *with* a person or thing

Indirect Object. An indirect object is a noun or pronoun that comes between an action verb and the direct object.

            IO   DO
Example: John threw *Joe* the *ball.*

The indirect object is always the receiver of the direct object and usually tells to whom or for whom the action of the verb is done.

Example: Mother baked *Mary* a *cake.* Ask — "Mother baked what?" Answer — *"a cake."* Cake is the direct object. Then ask — "To or for whom?" Answer — *"Mary."* Mary is the indirect object.

Remember this important hint: A sentence can have a direct object but no indirect object. *A sentence cannot have an indirect object without a direct object.* Also, the indirect object will *always* come between the action verb and the direct object.

Library Aids. Libraries are collections of books, periodicals, records, and microfilms arranged to make locating what is needed easy. They are inexhaustible sources of information and pleasure.
    The books in a library are grouped according to subject. Most *fiction,* particularly full-length novels, are arranged alphabetically by author's last name. *Non-fiction* and other fictional forms are arranged by a combination of numbers and letters according to one of two systems. The two most widely used classification systems and two common library aids are described in the following four subsections.

Card Catalog. Every library has a card catalog, the central file which may be used to locate any book in the collection. There are generally three cards for each book: an author card, a title card, and a subject card. All cards are arranged in the catalog drawers in alphabetical order. Usually subject cards are in one catalog while author and title cards fill another. The number in the upper left-hand corner of each card is the call number. The call numbers are determined by the Dewey Decimal system. Sample cards might look like the following:

22

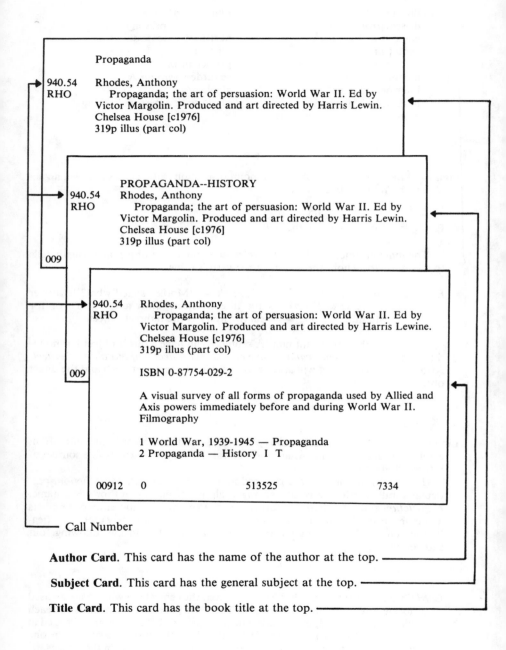

Propaganda

940.54 Rhodes, Anthony
RHO   Propaganda; the art of persuasion: World War II. Ed by
        Victor Margolin. Produced and art directed by Harris Lewin.
        Chelsea House [c1976]
        319p illus (part col)

009

PROPAGANDA--HISTORY
940.54 Rhodes, Anthony
RHO   Propaganda; the art of persuasion: World War II. Ed by
        Victor Margolin. Produced and art directed by Harris Lewin.
        Chelsea House [c1976]
        319p illus (part col)

009

940.54 Rhodes, Anthony
RHO   Propaganda; the art of persuasion: World War II. Ed by
        Victor Margolin. Produced and art directed by Harris Lewine.
        Chelsea House [c1976]
        319p illus (part col)

009   ISBN 0-87754-029-2

        A visual survey of all forms of propaganda used by Allied and
        Axis powers immediately before and during World War II.
        Filmography

        1 World War, 1939-1945 — Propaganda
        2 Propaganda — History I T

00912   0   513525   7334

— Call Number

Author Card. This card has the name of the author at the top. ──

Subject Card. This card has the general subject at the top. ──

Title Card. This card has the book title at the top. ──

Dewey Decimal System. The Dewey Decimal System is used in most schools and public libraries. It divides all subjects about which books might be written into 10 main categories, spanning numbers in the hundreds:

000-099	General works (encyclopedias, newspapers, periodicals)
100-199	Philosophy (conduct, ethics, psychology)
200-299	Religion (Bibles, mythology)
300-399	Social sciences (economics, law, education, government)
400-499	Language (dictionaries, grammars, languages) (located in the English resource center)
500-599	Pure sciences (mathematics, physics, chemistry, astronomy)
600-699	Technology (engineering, radio, television, business, medicine)
700-799	Arts and recreation
800-899	Literature (poems, plays, essays, but not other fiction) (located in the English resource center)
900-999	History (history, travel, geography, biography) (located in the social studies resource center)

Each category is broken down into hundreds of subcategories so that an expert can tell from a book's *call number* exactly what it is about.

Library of Congress Classification System. The Library of Congress Classification System is preferred in most college, university, and research libraries. In this system, the major subject classes are indicated by letters of the alphabet followed by numbers.

Reader's Guide to Periodical Literature. The *Reader's Guide* is an excellent guide to material for reports or pleasure reading. It leads readers directly to magazine articles on almost any topic. To use the *Reader's Guide*:

1. Look up the desired subject — subject entries are in alphabetical order and in capital letters.

2. A "See" or "See also" following the subject means helpful information can be found under the related subject listed after the "See".

3. All abbreviations are explained in two lists at the front of each *Reader's Guide.*

Example:

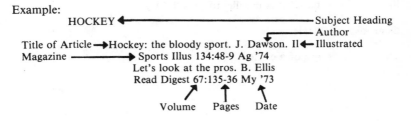

Mathematical Symbols. The following are symbols frequently used in mathematics and the sciences, and sometimes are also used in technical writing:

+	plus; positive (a + b = c) used also to indicate omitted figures or an approximation
−	minus; negative
±	plus or minus (the square root of $4a^2$ is ± 2a)
×	multiplied by; times (6 × 3 = 18). Writing factors other than numerals without signs (ab = cd) also indicates multiplication.
÷ or $\frac{a}{b}$ or a/b	divided by (24 ÷ 8 = 3) also indicated by writing the divisor under the dividend with a line between $\frac{24}{6}$ = 4 or by writing the divisor after the dividend with an oblique line between (3/4).
=	equals
≠ or ≠	is not equal to
>	is greater than (6 > 5)
<	is less than (3 < 4)
≧ ≥	is greater than or equal to
≦ ≤	is less than or equal to
≈	equivalent; similar
:	is to; the ratio of; such that
∴	therefore
∞	infinity
∠	angle; the angle (∠ ABC)
⊥	the perpendicular; is perpendicular to (AB ⊥ CD)
‖	parallel; is parallel to (AB ‖ CD)
⊙ or ○	circle
⌒	arc of a circle

$\sqrt{\ }$ or $\sqrt{\ }$	radical — used without a figure to indicate a square root (as in $\sqrt{4} = 2$) or with an index above the sign to indicate the root to be taken (as $\sqrt[3]{x}$) if the root is not a square root. $\sqrt{9}$ means find one of two equal factors of 9 (± 3). $\sqrt[3]{27}$ means find one of three equal factors of 27 (3).
( )	parentheses
[ ]	brackets
{ }	braces
U	union of two sets
∩	intersection of two sets
⊂	is included in, is a subset of
⊃	contains as a subset
∈	is an element of
∧ or ○ or ∅	empty set, null set
3.333	numbers beneath the bar indicate an infinite repetition of these numbers.
≅	in congruent to

Noun. A noun names a person, place, or thing, a quality, idea, or action. Nouns may be classified as *common* or *proper*; *abstract* or *concrete*; and *collective*.

A *proper* noun is the name of a particular person, place, or thing. They should be capitalized: Cathy, Germany, New York City.

A *common* noun does not name a particular person, place, or thing. Common nouns are not capitalized: man, state, officer.

An *abstract* noun names a quality, a characteristic, an idea: honesty, truth, goodness.

A *concrete* noun names an object which can be perceived by the senses: book, sweater, car, envelope.

A *collective* noun names a group: club, family, union, audience.

Noun Plurals. Many people find it fairly easy to spell the singular (meaning "one") of a word, but have trouble forming and correctly spelling plurals (meaning "more than one"). This might be expected, since many English words form plurals in unusual ways. A dictionary may be consulted for the proper spelling of the plural of any word. Common rules for forming plurals of nouns are:

1. Most nouns are regular, forming their plurals with *s*:

needles	books	toys
pins	judges	chairs

2. Nouns ending in *ch, sh, s, x,* and *z* add *es*:

churches	gases	taxes	Joneses
bushes	crosses	waltzes	birches

3. Nouns ending in *y* preceded by a consonant change the *y* to *i* and add *es*:

lady — ladies	memory — memories
penny — pennies	city — cities

4. Nouns ending in *y* preceded by a vowel add an *s*:

monkey — monkeys	donkey — donkeys

5. Nouns ending in *o* preceded by a vowel add *s*:

rodeo — rodeos	igloo — igloos	radio — radios
cameo — cameos	taboo — taboos	studio — studios

6. Nouns ending in *o* preceded by a consonant vary. Some add *s*, others *es*, and still others can use either *s* or *es*. These are often confusing and should be checked in a dictionary.

   Examples with *s*: piano — pianos, solo — solos, soprano — sopranos

   Examples with *es*: echo — echoes, hero — heroes, tomato — tomotoes, potato — potatoes

   Examples with *s* or *es*: hobo — hobos or hoboes, cargo — cargo or cargoes

7. Most nouns ending in *f* or *fe* are regular and add *s*. But some form plurals by changing the *f* or *fe* to *ve* and adding *s*.

   Examples with *s*: roof — roofs, dwarf — dwarfs, life — lifes

   Examples with *ves*: self — selves, knife — knives, life — lives, thief — thieves, half — halves, leaf — leaves

   Examples with *s* or *ves*: hoof — hoofs or hooves, scarf — scarfs or scarves

27

8. A few nouns form their plurals by a change in spelling.

child — children   ox — oxen
woman — women   louse — lice
mouse — mice   foot — feet
tooth — teeth   freshman — freshmen

9. Some nouns borrowed from foreign languages have English endings, others foreign endings, and still others have both:

Examples of English plurals: bonus — bonuses, campus — campuses, forum — forums encyclopedia — encyclopedias

Examples of Foreign plurals: alumnus — alumni, crisis — crises, alumna — alumnae, chateau — chateaux oasis — oases

Examples of both: index — indexes or indices, amoeba — amoebas or amoebae, beau — beaus or beaux, formula — formulas or formulae, appendix — appendices or appendixes

In scientific and formal writing the foreign plurals of words that have both forms are more likely to be used. But in other situations the English plurals are more common and are the appropriate forms to use. Consult a dictionary to be certain.

10. Compound nouns vary. When the compound is written as one word, the plural is formed by adding *s* or *es*:

cupful — cupfuls   leftover — leftovers
handful — handfuls   teaspoonful — teaspoonfuls
strongbox — strongboxes

When the parts are separate or hyphenated, the principal word is usually made plural:

man-of-war — men-of-war   brother-in-law — brothers-in-law
hanger-on — hangers-on   poet laureate — poets laureate
board of education — boards of   secretary-general — secretaries-
  education   general

The plurals of some compound nouns are formed in irregular ways:

drive-in — drive-ins
standby — standbys
four-year-old — four-year-olds

11. Letters, numbers, signs, and words discussed as words usually add *'s*:

   Examples: two *c's* and three *o's*, five 6's, three *q's*

   Don't use so many *and's, so's,* and *I's* in writing your paper.

   You have four *that's* in the first sentence.

   My last paper was full of *o's*, not + *'s*.

12. A few nouns have the same form for both singular and plural:

deer	athletics	slacks
fowl	politics	bellows
sheep	scissors	trout
elk	gallows	species

Noun Uses. The noun can appear in a wide variety of positions in a sentence.

Examples:	Subject	The *boy* ran.
	Object of Preposition	The boy ran after the *ball*.
	Direct Object	The boy hit the *ball*.
	Indirect Object	The boy threw *John* the ball.
	Appositive	The boy, a *student* at SPASH, plays golf.
	Predicate Noun	The boy is a *student*.

See *Subject, Object of Preposition, Direct Object, Indirect Object, Appositive,* and *Predicate Noun.*

Numbers. In ordinary writing, numbers that can be expressed in one or two words are generally spelled out; other numbers are usually written in figures.

Examples: Hortense canned *five* bushels of kumquats.
There are *twenty-four* sophomores in the club.
Reginald has *666* pennies to contribute.
We drove *three hundred* miles on the first day.

A number at the beginning of a sentence should always be written out:

Examples: *Four hundred fifty-two* students graduated last year.
Thirty percent of the students got A's.

Hyphenate all compound numbers from *twenty-one* to *ninety-nine* and fractions used as adjectives:

Examples: He spent *twenty-one* days in prison.
A *two-thirds* majority voted in favor of the amendment.

The form in which numbers are written should be consistent. If one of two or more numbers in a sentence cannot be expressed in two words or less, figures are used for all:

Example: In his piggy bank Jasper had *157* pennies, *83* nickels, *71* dimes, and *3* quarters.

Fractions written alone should be spelled out, but those which accompany a whole number should be expressed in figures.

Example: *One-fourth* ate at school regularly, but over *2½* times as many went home.

Numbers including decimals should always be expressed in figures. The word *percent* should be written out except in scientific writing where the % sign is used.

Style conventions for writing numbers may vary. So in any situation check for agreed-upon style rules.

Object of Preposition. An object of a preposition is a noun or pronoun that follows a preposition:

P   OP

Example: The boy ran *after the ball.*

The prepositional phrase can appear anywhere in the sentence. The noun or pronoun at the end of a prepositional phrase is the object of the preposition which begins the phrase.

P   OP

Examples: *Behind the house* stood an old oak tree.

P   OP

Mary went *to the store* yesterday.

P   OP

John hit the ball *over the fence.*

Parentheses (   ). There are three occasions when parentheses are called for in writing:

1. To enclose added explanations or comments that you do not want to stand out conspicuously within a sentence.

   Example: Three of the team (Sally, Lois, and Jenny) tried for the Most Valuable Player award.

   Punctuation marks (commas, periods, semicolons, etc.) that belong to the sentence come after the parentheses, not before.

   Example: Since Rob had never attended a wedding dance (he came from a small urban family), he didn't want to miss this one.

2. To add parenthetical material that is not in the body of a sentence. A capital letter and a period (or question mark or exclamation mark) should occur within the parentheses.

   Example: Mr. Stroik looked at me disapprovingly. (He always looks at me disapprovingly.) Then he said, "Where have you been this time?"

3. To enclose letters or figures that mark items in a series:

   Example: Mr. Hurst had three choices: (1) he could buy Tom the bike, (2) he could promise Tom the bike next year, or (3) he could say that Tom should buy his own bike.

   Parentheses are effective only when they are used occasionally. If used too often they become tiresome and distracting.

Parenthetical Material. A word, phrase, clause or sentence which is inserted in or added to a statement grammatically complete without it is known as a parenthetical. Such material is usually enclosed by marks of parentheses, commas, or dashes.
Example: Cathy's answer, *on the other hand*, was entirely correct.
The moral, *if there is a moral*, is that crime doesn't pay.
However, your analysis is correct.

Period (.). A period is used:

1. At the end of sentences that make statements, requests, or give commands.

2. After an abbreviation.

Possessives. Possessives are formed to show ownership.

Examples: dog's bone
boy's coat
ladies' coats

There are a few rules to follow that indicate where the apostrophe (') should be placed in the possessive word:

1. *Singular.* If the possessive word is singular, simply write the word and add apostrophe and *s* ('s).

Examples: witch's hat, spider's web, monkey's uncle, princess's crown

If the possessive noun is singular and ends in *s*, add either *'s,* or ' only. *Charles's* tonsils were larger than *Mrs. Jones's.* Or *Charles'* Honda was faster than *Mr. Jones'* tricycle.

Note: After you have chosen a form, use it consistently.

2. *Plural.* If the possessive word is plural and ends in *s*, simply add an apostrophe (').

Examples: farms' acreage, crops' storage bins, cows' stanchions, girls' stopwatch, coats' sleeves

If the possessive word is plural and does *not* end in *s*, add an apostrophe and an *s*.

Examples: women's fashions, children's books, oxen's carts, geese's feathers

Singular	*Singular Possessive*	*Plural*	*Plural Possessive*
boy	boy's	boys	boys'
roof	roof's	roofs	roofs'
ox	ox's	oxen	oxen's
dress	dress's	dresses	dresses'

For possessive case of pronouns, see *Pronouns.*

Predicate. The verb or verb phrase in a sentence which makes a statement — an assertion, an action, a condition, a state of being — about the subject is called the predicate. A *simple predicate* is a verb or a verb phrase alone, without an object or modifiers; a *complete predicate* consists of the verb with its object and all its modifiers; a *compound predicate* consists of two or more verbs or verb phrases.

Predicate Adjective. A predicate adjective is an adjective in the predicate part of the sentence. It follows a linking verb, not an action verb, and it will always describe a noun in the subject part of the sentence.

```
                S   LV  PA
Example:  My mother is pretty.
             S      LV  PA
          The cake smells good.
          Adj.  S      LV  PA
          The fresh cake smells good.
```

The following are sentences containing predicate nouns and predicate adjectives. Notice the difference between a predicate noun and a predicate adjective.

```
                                  PA
Examples:  1. The little girl appeared sick.
                             PN
           2. That boy is a thief.
                                PA
           3. Mrs. Jones seems crabby.
                        PA
           4. We are so happy.
                              PN
           5. SPASH is a good school.
                              PN
           6. Jim became president of his class.
```

Predicate *adjectives* describe. Predicate *nouns* rename. A predicate *adjective* never modifies a predicate noun.

```
            S   LV   Adj.  PN
Example:  Star Wars is a favorite movie.
```
The adjective *favorite* is not a predicate adjective.

See *Predicate Noun.*

Predicate Noun. A predicate noun is a noun in the predicate part of the sentence. It follows a linking verb, not an action verb, and it will always rename a noun in the subject part of a sentence.

```
              S   LV   PN
Examples:  My mother is a teacher.
            S  LV LV    PN
           Susan will be a lawyer.
            S  LV     PN
           Ann was a witch (in the school play).
           LV   S    PN
           Was George a student?
```

Following is a list of the linking verbs. These will help in recognizing predicate nouns and predicate adjectives.

Linking Verbs

be	was	become	taste
am	were	appear	feel
is	been	seem	sound
are	being	look	smell
stay	grow	remain	

Prefixes. A syllable or syllables can be added to the beginning of a word to change the meaning (as *dis* in *disinherit*) or modify the meaning (as *pre* in *preview*). These prefixes are one of the elements that make up many words, others being suffixes and roots. Most English prefixes have their origin in Greek or Latin. It will help, to figure out the meaning of many words, to know what some of the common prefixes mean. All prefixes are listed in the dictionary.

GREEK PREFIXES

Affix	*Meaning*	*Examples*
phil	loving, fond of	philosopher, bibliophile
mis	hate (opposite of phil)	misanthrope
dys	bad, ill, difficult	dysentery, dystrophy
eu	good, well (opposite of dys)	eulogize, euthanasia
a, an	not, without	amoral, anemia
mono	one, single, alone	monarchy, monosyllabic
poly	many	polyarchy, polysyllabic
homo	one, the same, like	homonym, homochromatic
hetero	different	heteronym, heterochromatic
morph	form	amorphous, metamorphosis

LATIN PREFIXES

Affix	*Meaning*	*Examples*
ab	away	abduct, abnormal
ad	toward, to	adjourn, administer
anti	against	anti-aircraft
bi	two	biped, binomial
co	with	cooperate, coauthor
com, con	with	concur, combine
dis	reverse of	disobey, disadvantage
ex	out of	excavate, exclude
extra	beyond, outside	extraordinary, extrasensory
in	into, not	include, incapable
inter	together, between	intertwine
intra	within	intramural, intracardiac
mis	bad, wrong	misadventure, mistake
non	no	nonaligned, nonsense
post	after	postgraduate, postoperative
pre, pro	before, forth	prepare, project
re	back, again	regress, reread
semi	half	semiconscious, semiskilled
sub	under	subconscious, subcutaneous
super	above, greater	superstructure, supertanker
trans	across	transportation, transatlantic

Prepositional Phrases. A prepositional phrase is made up of at least two words — a preposition and the first noun (or pronoun) following it. This noun (or pronoun) is called the object of the preposition.

Prep.   OP

Examples: The man walked *down the street.*

Prep.   OP

The rock band fell *through the floor.*

Prep.   OP

The girl *in the blue sweater* is my friend.

Prep. OP

Send this letter *to her.*

The object of a preposition may be compound.

Prep. OP   OP

Example: I sent the memo *to Phil and Marilyn.*

One way to remember most of the prepositions is to imagine a bee flying around a hive. Whatever he can do to show his relationship to the hive is a preposition.

Example: He can fly -- *under* the hive.
over the hive.
around the hive.
through the hive.
into the hive.

The prepositions are:

aboard	behind	in	since
about	below	inside	through
above	beside	into	throughout
across	between	like	to
after	beyond	near	toward
against	by	of	under
along	down	off	until
amid	during	on	underneath
among	except	out	unto
around	for	out of	upon
at	from	outside	up
as	from among	over	with
before	from between	past	within
beneath	from under	round	without

See also *Idioms.*

Pronouns. A pronoun is a word used in place of one or more nouns. There are three pronoun cases which indicate the relationship of the pronoun with other words in the sentence:

Nominative — used as subjects and predicate nouns

Objective — used as direct objects, indirect objects, and objects of the preposition

Possessive — used to show ownership

Examples:

	Nominative Case		Objective Case	
Person	Singular	Plural	Singular	Plural
1st	I	we	me	us
2nd	you	you	you	you
3rd	he, she, it	they	him, her, it	them

	Possessive Case	
Person	Singular	Plural
1st	my, mine	our, ours
2nd	your, yours	your, yours
3rd	his, her, hers, its	their, theirs

Pronouns, Agreement with Antecedent. A pronoun must agree with its *antecedent*, the noun to which the pronoun refers.

Example: Bob is nice. *He* is my friend.

Since *Bob* is the antecedent of *he*, the second sentence needs a masculine (not *she*), singular (not *they*), and nominative pronoun as the subject. There are a few rules to remember for pronouns and their antecedents, since they must agree with each other.

1. If the antecedent is singular, the pronoun must be singular. (These words are always singular: *each, either, neither, everyone, everybody, anyone, anybody, someone, somebody, nobody, no one,* and *one.*)

Example: *Someone* has left *his* book.

2. When an antecedent is modified by *each, every, either,* or *neither*, a singular pronoun must be used to agree with it.

Example: *Every* girl will bring *her* own gym suit.

3. If the antecedent is plural, the pronoun must be plural.

    Example: My *friends* left *their* books here.
    Joe and *Larry* will deliver *their* papers today.

4. In a sentence with *neither — nor* or *either — or* the pronoun must agree with the noun nearest to it.

    Example: Neither Don nor *Terry* will tell *his* secret.
    Either Bob or his *friends* will bring *their* books.

5. Sometimes a prepositional phrase comes between the antecedent and the pronoun. This can be confusing.

    Example: *Each* (of the girls) will tell *her* story.

6. When you can't tell whether an antecedent is masculine or feminine, use a masculine pronoun to agree with it.

    Example: *Everyone* should give *his* report on Monday.

Pronoun Types. Depending on how a pronoun is used in a sentence, it may be classified as one of the following:

Personal: Those listed under nominative and objective cases under *Pronouns*.

Possessive: Those listed under possessive case under *Pronouns*.

Demonstrative: *this, that, these, those*

Interrogative: *who, whose, whom, which, what*

Indefinite: *all, another, any, anybody, both, each, either, everyone, few, many, neither, none, nobody, several, someone*

Relative: *who, whom, which, that*

Reflexive: *myself, yourself, himself, herself, itself, ourselves, yourselves, themselves*

Question Mark (?). A question mark is used at the end of a sentence that asks questions. A question mark should not be used after an indirect question.

Example: *Wrong*: I was asked if I wanted to sing?
Right: I was asked if I wanted to sing.

A question mark may also be used to indicate a series of queries in the same sentence.

Example: Will she be here? on time? properly dressed?
Can she come? or her sister? or her parents?

But, the question mark should not be overused for this purpose. It is nearly always possible to find another way to phrase the sentence.

Quotation Marks (" "). Quotation marks are used:

1. To enclose the titles of poems, stories, songs, chapters, and articles.

2. To enclose a direct quotation.

    Examples: "I will leave," said Mary.
    Mary said, "I will leave."
    "Yes," replied Alice, "he is my brother."
    "Is he your teacher?" asked Jan.
    "Look out!" yelled Marge.

    Use single quotation marks for a quotation within a quotation.

    Example: "Of course, Louis said, 'Let Leon do it.' " Helen said with a sigh.

3. To set off unacceptable usage (rarely used).

    Example: I'm "boilin' mad" about the deal.

4. With other punctuation marks the period and comma fall within the quotation marks.

    Example: "I'm here," he shouted.

    A semi-colon falls outside the quotation marks.

    Example: He said, "I'm going Friday"; however, he didn't get away before Sunday.

    A dash, question mark, and exclamation point fall within quotation marks when they refer to the material quoted only. When they refer to the whole sentence they fall outside.

    Example: Why did Tom say, "I'm not going."?

Roots. Roots are words or parts of words from which other words can be formed. Many English roots also came from Greek and Latin. A common Greek root is *phone* or *phono*, which came from the Greek phone ("voice"). Such words as *telephone, phonetic, phonograph, megaphone,* and *microphone* are built on this root.

A few of the more common roots include:

Root	Meaning	Examples
graph	write	autograph, telegraph
phobia	fear	claustrophobia, musophobia
script	write	manuscript, description
spec	look	inspector, spectator

Semicolon (;). The semicolon is used to join two sentence structures not connected by a conjunction like *and, but, for,* or *or.*

Example: We'll have to hurry; it's almost seven o'clock.
Jeff laughed aloud; Doug smiled mysteriously; Russ just shook his head.

Semicolons are used to join two sentence structures that are connected by conjunctive adverbs like *however, moreover, therefore, for example, in other words.*

Example: Mr. Johnston said the decision is up to us; in other words, he will not assume responsibility for the outcome of our project.

Semicolons are used between the items in a series if any of the items contains a comma.

Examples: The members of the panel included Sue Ardmore, a Junior at SPASH; Mr. Josh Cahill, the principal of Wisconsin Rapids High School; and Dr. Mary Davies, a professor of English at the University of Wisconsin.

We also plan to visit several smaller cities: Achim, West Germany; Uppsala, Sweden; Stavenger, Norway; and Turku, Finland.

Sentence. A sentence is a group of words expressing a completed thought.

Example: *Sentence:* The lowest scores in the writing test were made by science majors.

Not a sentence: The lowest scores in the writing test made by science majors.

Sentences are classified according to their purpose and according to their structure.

Sentence, Arrangement of Content. Sentences may be grouped into three categories according to the arrangement of ideas within them.

1. Loose — A sentence in which the grammatical form and the basic idea are complete before the end of the sentence is revealed.

Basic Idea

Example: *Jerry slowly emptied the box of scraps* with bits of paper drifting quietly to the floor.

2. Balanced — A sentence in which two or more ideas of equal length and grammatical form are set opposite each other, usually on either side of a semicolon.

Basic Idea   Basic Idea

Example: *To err is human; to forgive [is] divine.*

3. Periodic — A sentence in which the main idea is not complete until the end.

Basic Idea

Example: Standing quietly by the door, his ticket in hand, *the boy waited for the bus.*

Sentence Errors. The basic errors in sentence structure may ge grouped into three categories: the fragment, the run-on, and the awkward sentence.

1. *Sentence Fragments.* A fragment is a group of words that does not sound complete. It usually does not tell who did something, what someone or something did, or what happened. When a fragment is read, it seems as if something is missing.

Example: *Walking at a brisk pace down the road.* At once the reader asks, "Who is walking?" The thought is incomplete. To make a fragment a sentence, the writer must complete the thought.

Fred was walking at a brisk pace down the road. This is a sentence because it expresses a complete thought.

2. *Run-On Sentences.* A run-on is simply two or more sentences run together or read together as one sentence because the writer has not punctuated the sentences correctly.

Example: Tom was late for school, he forgot to set his alarm.

Ordinarily, two independent statements are joined to form a single sentence with a conjunction (*and, but, or*) plus a comma or with a semicolon. If a comma alone is used to join these statements, however, a run-on sentence is the result. Run-ons are corrected as follows:

A. By using a subordinating conjunction to show that one idea depends on the other. (Tom was late for school *because* he forget to set his alarm.)

B. By using a conjunctive adverb (sentence connector) plus a semicolon to join the ideas. (Tom forgot to set his alarm; *therefore*, he was late for school.)

C. By using a semicolon alone. (Tom forgot to set his alarm; he arrived late for school.)

3. *Awkward Sentences.* The awkward sentence, the third type of sentence problem, is produced by a variety of difficulties in composing the sentence, but generally results in writing that is simply difficult to read. See the sections in this handbook dealing with *Dangling Modifiers,* and *Parallel Structure* for specific examples of the most common and awkward constructions.

Sentence Patterns. Grammar is simply a description of the system of *recurring sentence patterns* that make up the English language. In fact, all of the sentences that can possibly be written develop from the basic patterns listed below. These patterns are called *kernel* sentences because the more complex expressions we use in writing and speaking "grow" from these recurring basic patterns. The five basic sentence patterns include:

```
     S     V
1. Students read.          Subject-Verb: S-V
     S     V     O
2. Students buy books.     Subject-Verb-Object: S-V-O
     S     LV    C
3. Students are people.    Subject-Linking Verb-Noun Complement:
                           S-LV-NC
     S     LV    C
4. Students are young.     Subject-Linking Verb-Adjective Complement:
                           S-LV-AC
     S     LV    ADV
5. Students are nearby.    Subject-Linking Verb-Adverb: S-LV-ADV
```

Five less common sentence patterns include:

1. He gave me money. (Indirect Object Pattern)
2. They elected him president. (Objective Complement Pattern)
3. There is a man outside. (Expletive Pattern)
4. Where are you going? (Question Pattern)
5. The report was read by the chairman. (Passive Pattern)

One might well ask then, if all the possible sentences in the English language are derived from such simple patterns, how can some sentences become so long and elaborate? Actually, the process of writing longer sentences simply involves *combining* shorter ones whose ideas relate directly to each other. For example, take these two simple sentences and see what happens when they are combined.

Example: A. He went away. I have been unhappy.
             B. I have been unhappy since he went away.

Notice that in A, no relationship is shown between the ideas; the reader must *assume* a relationship, if any exists. However, a relationship is shown in combination B: He went away is the *cause* of the "unhappiness."

This process of combining short sentences into longer ones to show the relationships between ideas is called *sentence expansion,* and two basic principles are involved in the process. These principles are called *subordination* and *coordination* and require only that the writer decide how important the ideas are that he is combining. If the ideas to be combined are of *equal* value, we say they are *coordinate* and should be expressed in the same grammatical form (words, phrases, clauses). For example: "*John enjoys skin-diving, and Susan enjoys fishing.*" are coordinate ideas (of equal value) and, therefore, both are expressed as main clauses. Any language structures may be coordinated.

Example: John and Mary practice and enjoy sailing, swimming, and skin-diving.

On the other hand, if ideas to be combined are of *unequal value,* we say that the less important idea is *subordinate* to the other. For example, subordinate ideas may be combined with a main idea as follows:

Examples:

Base sentence	The tree shed its leaves.
Verbal Phrase Modifier	The tree *growing in my neighbor's yard* shed its leaves.
Prepositional Phrase Modifier	The tree *in my neighbor's yard* shed its leaves.
Single Word Modifier	The large *beech* tree shed its leaves.
Appositive	The tree, *a large beech in my neighbor's yard,* shed its leaves.

Sentence Structures. There are four types of sentence structures: *simple, compound, complex,* and *compound-complex.*

Simple Sentences. A simple sentence has one subject and one predicate. Either or both of these may be compound.

Examples: Jerry *ate* fourteen pickles.
The football team and the basketball squad *are* both at the banquet.
Sam and Judy *swam* and *picnicked* at Iverson Park.

Compound Sentences. A compound sentence is made up of two or more independent clauses or simple sentences. See also *Clauses.* If the clauses are joined by a conjunction (*and, but, or, nor*), a comma precedes the conjunction unless the sentence is very short.
The conjunction may be replaced by a semicolon in a compound sentence with two closely related clauses.

             Independent   Independent
Examples: Sue went shopping, and Sandra painted the bedroom.

            Independent   Independent
George gobbled the mushrooms; Dennis stuffed himself with tuna salad.

Complex Sentences. A complex sentence has one independent clause and one or more dependent clauses.
A dependent clause begins with a subordinate conjunction.

Subordinate Conjunctions

after	how	that	whenever
although	if	though	where
as	since	unless	whether
because	so	until	while
before	than	when	why

      Ind. Dependent
Examples: I heard (*that* he is sly).

     Dependent   Ind.   Dep.
(*Although* I understood his motives), I didn't feel (*that* he was justified).

If the dependent clause is at the beginning of the sentence, it is followed by a comma.

Compound-Complex Sentences. A compound-complex sentence consists of two or more independent clauses plus at least one dependent clause.

     Ind.   Dependent   Independent
Example: Bob knew (that Tim was at the game), but he tried to call him anyway.
     Dependent   Independent
(Although I was tired), I brought the homework to the teacher's
     Independent
desk and he checked it with me.

Spelling.

1. Adverbs ending in *ly* are formed directly by addition to the adjective.

2. Nouns ending in *ness* are formed directly by addition to the adjective.

3. Prefixes are written before words without doubling or dropping letters.

4. There is no word in English ending in *full* except the word *full* when it stands alone.

5. There are only three *ceed* words: *exceed, proceed,* and *succeed.*

6. Possessive pronouns are never written with an apostrophe because they are already in the possessive form.

7. Singular nouns form the possessive by adding an apostrophe and an *s*.

8. Plural nouns that do *not* end in *s* form the possessive by adding an apostrophe and an *s* (*men's hats*).

9. If *y* is preceded by a consonant, change the *y* to *i* before any suffix except *ing*. (*merciful, merriest, fancying*)

10. Use *i* before *e* except after *c* or when sounded like *ay* as in *neighbor* and *weigh*.

11. Words ending in *y* preceded by a consonant form the plural by changing the *y* to *i* and adding *es*.

12. Words ending in *y* preceded by a vowel form the plural by adding *s*.

13. Most nouns ending in *o* preceded by a consonant form the plural by adding *es*.

14. Nouns ending in *o* preceded by a vowel form the plural by adding *s*.

15. Most musical terms ending in *o* form the plural by adding *s*.

16. Most compound nouns form the plural by adding *s* to the principal word (*fathers-in-law, commanders-in-chief*).

17. Nouns ending in *s, x, z, sh,* and soft *ch* form the plural by adding *es*.

18. Drop the silent *e* before a suffix beginning with a vowel; retain the silent *e* before a suffix beginning with a consonant.

19. Sound correctly any long words; then break them into syllables and spell the "shorter words."

44

Subject. The subject of a sentence is the word or group of words in the sentence about which the predicate makes a statement or question. It is the person, place, or thing the sentence is talking about.

Most of the time, the subject will come before the verb: The *boy ran.*

Sometimes the subject will follow the verb: There *is mother.*

Usually the subject will follow the verb in a sentence that asks a question:

V   S

Where *is* my *mother?*

The complete subject is the subject and all the words (modifiers, etc.) that belong to it.

Example: *The grinning barbarian, his teeth clenched,* looked into the barn yard.
"Barbarian" is the simple subject; the first six words make the complete subject.

Examples: *Miss Click's class* is serving carrot fudge to the football team today.
He who hesitates gets bumped from the rear.

The verb can be any of the twenty-three helping verbs plus, if there is one, an action or being word. The verb can also be a single action or being word.

Examples: The team *had started* their warm-up.
Our school choir *will be singing* next.
I *am* not *going* with you.
He *is* sick.
Did he *finish* the project?

Usually the subject comes before the verb. Sometimes, however, it will come after the verb.

Examples: There *is* Jane.
Behind the door *was* a secret passage.

In the above examples, subjects are circled and verbs italicized.

Subject-Verb Agreement. A verb must agree with its subject.

1. If the subject has two or more nouns joined by *and*, use a verb that means more than one.

    Example: *Bob* and *Tom are* having trouble sleeping because of indigestion.

2. If the subject is joined by *or* or *nor*, the verb agrees with the part of the subject nearer the verb. Verbs agreeing with singular subjects usually end in *s*.

   Examples: Either the girls or *Jack has* the ancient secret.
   Neither Grunhilda nor the *students notice* the werewolf leaping through the kitchen window until it is too late.

3. Do not be misled by a phrase that comes between the subject and the verb. The verb agrees with the subject, not with a noun or a pronoun in the phrase.

   Examples: The *subject* of his remarks *was* the sleigh parked on the roof.
   The *costs* of the flight to Pluto *have* increased.

4. Expressions such as *with, together with, including, accompanied by, in addition to,* or *as well as* do not change the number of the subject. If the subject is singular, the verb must refer to only one.

   Examples: *Mary*, as well as her brothers, *swings* through the branches with ease.
   Mrs. Brown, accompanied by her Camel Athletic Club, *was* present.

5. The words *each, each one, either, neither, everyone, everybody, anybody,* and *nobody* are singular and require a verb that agrees.

   Examples: *Neither* of the girls *has* any interest in Uncle Snerdley's hobby.

6. Sentences beginning with *there* are usually inverted in order. Be sure the verb agrees with the subject. *There* is never the subject of a sentence.

   Examples: There *are* many *birds* in the trees.
   There *is* only one *detour* on that route.

Suffixes. Suffixes are words or parts of words added to the end of another word or word root to form a new word or to form an inflectional ending, as *ness* in *gentleness* or *ing* in *walking*.

Suffix	Meaning	Example
ant	one who is	servant, inhabitant
er	one who does	buyer, seller
ist	one who believes in	typist, deist
or	one who does	operator
ful	full of	beautiful, remorseful
ic	like	fantastic, demonic
ish	like	foolish

Suffix	*Meaning*	*Example*
ize	to cause to become	standardize, popularize
less	without	hopeless, shapeless
ly	in the manner	quietly, disgustingly
sion	process of or state of being	expulsion, depression
tion	process of or state of being	rejection, elation
ward	in the direction of	homeward
hood	condition of	childhood, adulthood
ness	condition of	foolishness

Synonyms. A word having the same meaning as another, or nearly the same meaning as another word is a synonym.

Examples: cold, chill
hotel, inn, tavern
rescue, save, redeem

Although the meanings of synonyms may be very close, they are slightly different. Choose carefully which best fits the meaning and style of the sentence. In the following sentence, for example, *rescue* is the most appropriate of the three synonyms. *Save* might also be used, but *redeem* would be inappropriate.

Example: Joe is trying to *rescue* the drowning sheep.

Improve your command of synonyms by observing and using the words that you come across in reading and conversation. When you need a synonym for a specific word, use a special reference book such as:

Webster's Dictionary of Synonyms
Funk and Wagnall's Standard Handbook of Synonyms
Antonyms and Prepositions
Roget's International Thesaurus
The New Roget's Thesaurus of the English Language in Dictionary Form

The first two not only list synonyms but make clear what their different connotations are, giving the distinctions between them.

Underlining. Underlining is used to show that a word is used in a special way. In printed materials *italics* are used instead of underlining.

1. Underline the titles of books, magazines, newspapers, long poems, plays, compositions, movies, the names of ships, aircraft, spacecraft, and works of art. (Use quotation marks for title of chapters, stories, short poetry, or articles in books or magazines.)

Example: He flew on Jetline's <u>Phantom Whisper II</u> to see the <u>Mona Lisa</u>.

2. Underline a word referred to as a word or a letter as a letter.

    Example: Don't forget the p in psychology.

3. Underline foreign words and phrases:

    Example: If you study Latin, you'll understand the phrase e pluribus unum on your coins.

See also *Science Reports and Papers* for uses of underlining in scientific names.

Verb. A verb is a word which shows action (*run*) or a state of being (*am*). You can easily recognize an action verb. To learn the being verbs, check a list of auxiliary and linking verbs. See also *Verb Types.* You may also try to use a word in the following sentence to identify the word as a verb. Most verbs will satisfactorily complete the sentence:

Let's _____ it.

The forms of the verb show *tense* (or time). These forms, called the four principal parts of a verb, are the *present tense, present participle, past tense,* and *past participle.* The present and past participle must always have auxiliary verbs before them. You can remember these parts of a verb by learning the following sentences:

Present Tense	*Today* I sing, go, run, etc.
Present Participle	*Today* I *am* singing, going, running, etc.
Past Tense	*Yesterday* I sang, went, ran, etc.
Past Participle	I *have* sung, gone, run, etc. many times before.

Verbs, Irregular and Regular. A verb can be *regular* or *irregular* depending on how the principal parts are formed. A regular verb forms its past and past participle by adding *d* or *ed* to the present (*walk, walked, walked*).

Sometimes the end of a verb must be changed before the *d* or *ed* is added. Remember these rules:

1. If a regular verb of one syllable, or of more than one syllable with the accent on the last syllable, ends in a single consonant preceded by a single vowel, the consonant is doubled before *ed* is added (*step, stepped; omit, omitted*).

Present	*Past*	*Past Participle*	*Present*	*Past*	*Past Participle*
ask	asked	asked	dim	dimmed	dimmed
attack	attacked	attacked	drop	dropped	dropped
attach	attached	attached	stop	stopped	stopped
help	helped	helped	tan	tanned	tanned
pass	passed	passed	try	tried	tried
bat	batted	batted	cry	cried	cried

2. An irregular verb forms its past and past participle in other ways than by adding *d* or *ed* to the present. A list of irregular verbs follows. (Some of these verbs do have *d* or *ed* added to the present. However, they are often misused and are a little more difficult than the other regular verbs. Watch them carefully.)

Present	Past	Past Participle	Present	Past	Past Participle
am	was	been	bring	brought	brought
awake	awoke, awaked	awoke	burn	burned, burnt	burned
awaken	awakened	awakened	burst	burst	burst
bear	bore	borne, born	buy	bought	bought
			catch	caught	caught
beat	beat	beaten	choose	chose	chosen
become	became	become	climb	climbed	climbed
begin	began	begun	come	came	come
bend	bent	bent	cost	cost	cost
bid	bade, bid	bid, bidden	creep	crept	crept
			dig	dug	dug
bite	bit	bitten	dive	dived, dove	dived
blow	blew	blown			
break	broke	broken	do	did	done
drag	dragged	dragged	put	put	put
draw	drew	drawn	raise	raised	raised
drink	drank	drunk	ride	rode	ridden
drive	drove	driven	ring	rang	rung
drown	drowned	drowned	rise	rose	risen
drug	drugged	drugged	run	ran	run
eat	ate	eaten	say	said	said
fall	fell	fallen	see	saw	seen
fight	fought	fought	sell	sold	sold
find	found	found	set	set	set
flee	fled	fled	sew	sewed	sewn, sewed
fling	flung	flung	shake	shook	shaken
flow	flowed	flowed	shine	shone, shined	shone
fly	flew	flown			
forget	forgot	forgotten, forgot	show	showed	shown, showed
forgive	forgave	forgiven	shrink	shrank	shrunk
freeze	froze	frozen	sing	sang	sung
get	got	got (gotten)	sink	sank	sunk
			sit	sat	sat
give	gave	given	slay	slew	slain
go	went	gone	sleep	slept	slept
grow	grew	grown	slide	slid	slid
hang	hung, hanged	hung, hanged	sling	slung	slung
			sneak	sneaked	sneaked
have	had	had	sow	sowed	sown, sowed
hear	heard	heard			
heat	heated	heated	speak	spoke	spoken

Present	Past	Past Participle	Present	Past	Past Participle
hide	hid	hidden	spend	spent	spent
hold	held	held	spring	sprang	sprung
hurt	hurt	hurt	stand	stood	stood
keep	kept	kept	steal	stole	stolen
kneel	knelt	knelt	sting	stung	stung
know	knew	known	strike	struck	struck
lay	laid	laid	study	studied	studied
lead	led	led	sweep	swept	swept
learn	learned	learned	swim	swam	swum
leave	left	left	swing	swung	swung
lend	lent	lent	take	took	taken
let	let	let	teach	taught	taught
lie	lay	lain	tear	tore	torn
(rest)			tell	told	told
lie	lied	lied	think	thought	thought
(fib)			throw	threw	thrown
lose	lost	lost	wake	waked,	waked,
make	made	made		woke	woken
mean	meant	meant	wear	wore	worn
meet	met	met	win	won	won
mistaken	mistook	mistaken	wind	wound	wound
pay	paid	paid	write	wrote	written

Verb Mood. The form of the verb indicating the way in which the writer regards the sentence is the *mood* of the verb. Three types of mood are:

1. *Indicative Mood* — Used to make statements regarded as facts.

   Example: The school *will be* closed on Saturday.

2. *Imperative Mood* — Used to make statements regarded as commands.

   Example: *Close* the door!

3. *Subjunctive Mood* — Used to make statements regarded as doubtful, wishful, or contrary to fact. The statements are often introduced by *if* or *as though* and make use of the subjunctive *were*.

   Example: *If* he *were* here, you could discuss the issues with him.

Verb Tenses. The form of the verb shows the time (tense) of the action expressed in sentences. Six tenses are commonly used in English to designate actions as occurring in the past, present, or future.

50

1. *Present tense* is the base form of the verb used (a) to express an action occurring at the present time, or (b) to express a general truth, regardless of time.

   Examples: I *live* in Stevens Point.
   Students *enjoy* vacations.

2. *Past tense* is formed regularly* by adding *d* or *ed* to the base form of the verb and expressing an action that occurred in the past but did not continue into the present.

   Example: I *lived* in Stevens Point.

3. *Future tense* is formed with the words *will* or *shall* and expressing an action that will occur in the future.

   Example: I *will live* in Stevens Point.

   Note: The present tense forms of the verb used with an adverb indicating time may also be used to show future actions.

   Example: The assignment *is due* on *Friday*.

4. *Present perfect tense* is formed with the words *have* or *has* and expressing an action begun in the past and extending into the present.

   Example: Bill *has complained* about the work for an hour.

5. *Past perfect tense* is formed with the word *had* and expressing an action completed in the past before some other past action.

   Example: When I *had discussed* the problem with him completely, he went home.

6. *Future perfect tense* is formed with *will have* or *shall have* and is used to express an action to be completed in the future *before* some other future action.

   Example: By the end of football season, he *will have lost* twenty pounds.

7. *Progressive form*, a variation of the tenses listed above, consists of the helping verb *be* and the present participle (ing*) used in expressing a continuing action.

   Example: I *am thinking* carefully about the problem.

*Some verbs called irregular verbs, do not show tense by adding *d, ed*, or *ing*. See also *Verbs, Irregular and Regular.*

Verb Types. Verbs are often classified into types:

1. *Transitive Verbs.* A verb is called transitive when it is used with a direct object to complete its meaning.

   Trans. DO
   Example: Tom *threw* the *ball.*

2. *Intransitive Verbs.* A verb is called intransitive when it is used without a direct object to complete its meaning.

   Intrans.
   Example: Sally *left* early today. (No direct object)

3. *Linking Verbs.* A verb used to connect a subject with an adjective or noun in the predicate that describes or means the same as the subject is called a linking verb.

   Link.
   Examples: She *is* the best writer. (Links subject *She* to predicate noun *writer*)

   Link.
   Tom *was* late. (Links subject *Tom* to predicate adjective *late*)

   Forms of *be (am, is, are, was, were)* are the most common linking verbs. Other verbs frequently used as linking verbs and sometimes called "state of being" verbs include *act, appear, become, feel, go, grow, look, run, seem, smell, taste,* and *turn.*

   State/being
   Example: Jerry *seems* lazy today. (Links subject *Jerry* to predicate adjective *lazy*)

4. *Auxiliary Verbs.* Auxiliary verbs, sometimes called helping verbs, combine with main verbs to show tense, mood, or voice.

   Aux. MV
   Examples: George *is swimming* at SPASH. (present progressive tense)

   Aux. MV
   The whale *was tossed* by the waves. (passive voice)

   Aux. MV
   Mabel *will claim* the victory. (future tense)

   Aux. Aux. MV
   Ms. Jones *had been doing* the writing. (past perfect progressive tense)

Twenty-three auxiliaries are used in English in various combinations:

am	be	has	may	do
is	being	have	might	does
are	been	had	must	did
was	shall	will	can	
were	should	would	could	

52

Voice of Verbs. Voice is a form of the verb which indicates whether the subject of the sentence performs the action of the verb or receives the action of the verb.

Examples: Active voice — John *read* the book.
Passive voice — The book *was read* by John.

The passive verb is formed by combining a form of *be (am, is, are, was, were)* with the past participle (ed).

In most sentences the active verb is preferable because it is more forceful and direct. In addition, a shift from the active to the passive voice within the same sentence or even the same paragraph should be avoided.

Examples: Poor — The players warmed up *as the court was encircled by the cheerleaders* and the band played. (passive)
Better — The players warmed up *as the cheerleaders encircled the court* and the band played. (active)

Verbals. Verbals are forms of verbs that are used as nouns, adjectives, or adverbs. There are three types: participle, gerund, infinitive.

Participle. A participle may occur in the present participle form (verb plus *ing*), the past participle form (verb plus *ed*), or irregular past tense form *(worn, slept, sunk).* The participle is always used as an adjective.

Examples: The *swimming* hole owned by Mr. Zdroik was a popular spot.
Founded in 1862, the school maintained its traditions proudly.
The branches *swaying* in the breeze are beautiful.
The girl expertly *riding* the horse is named Joan.
They found the baby *crying.*

Note: Ask "who" or "what" about the participle to find the word it modifies.

Gerund. Like the participle, a gerund is a verb form often ending in *ing*, but it is used as a *noun.*

Examples: *Sailing* a boat is a good sport. (The gerund *sailing* names an action.)
Sailing merrily along, he forgot the day's worries. (The participle *sailing* modifies *he.*)

The gerund has the same uses as a noun.

Examples: *Eating* is enjoyable. (subject)
He is tired of *walking.* (object of preposition)
She hated *dieting.* (direct object)
He gave *skiing* a bad name. (indirect object)
Her favorite sport is *swimming.* (predicate noun)
His first love, *playing* tennis, is an exciting sport. (appositive)

Infinitive. The infinitive is the present tense form of the verb preceded by the word *to.* The infinitive may be used as a noun, adjective, or adverb.

Examples: *To fight* bravely is our goal. (subject)
He wanted *to attend.* (direct object)
To see is *to believe.* (predicate noun)
His goal, *to ski* well, was realized. (appositive)
She is a person *to be admired.* (adjective modifying "person")
They came *to ask* his advice. (adverb modifying "came")

In most cases, verbals do not occur as single words but rather as *phrases* with other associated words. Since the verbal maintains its verb character even though it is being used as an adjective, adverb, or noun, it may:

A. be modified by an adverb.
B. take a direct object.
C. take a predicate noun or predicate adjective.

Therefore, any of the preceding words would be included as a part of the verbal phrase.

Examples: He began *to swim slowly.* ("Slowly" is an adverb modifying "to swim" and is a part of the infinitive phrase.)
She tried *tying her shoes.* ("Her shoes" is the direct object of "tying" and is therefore part of the gerund phrase.)

Dangling Modifiers. A modifier that has no word in the sentence which it can sensibly modify is said to be dangling. This situation, often occurring with participles, is corrected by supplying a noun to be modified by the participle.

Examples: Dangling — After taking a shower, the bathroom floor usually has to be mopped up by Clint.
Revised — After taking a shower, Clint usually has to mop up the bathroom floor.

Dangling — At the age of six, Judy's father sold his potato farm and bought a snowmobile dealership.
Revised — When Judy was six, her father sold his potato farm and bought a snowmobile dealership.

54

Part II: Principles of Writing

Dialect. Although the sentence is the basic unit of expression, confusion sometimes results from the variety of writing styles and language choices available to the writer. The very richness of our language and the complexities of the communication situation can cause difficulties in knowing what types of sentences to use. Different situations raise different expectations about what kinds of sentence structure are acceptable. In speech, in advertising, in fiction, and in expository writing, the word choices and degree of sentence completeness differ.

Speech, because of its spontaneous nature, is often made up of incomplete sentences, gestures that substitute for words, and special language usages that are unique to the part of the country and cultural background of the area. In Central Wisconsin you might hear, "Come down by my house after school." Or "What's her name from home?" Used in informal conversation these would be easily understood, particularly if accompanied by the gestures and facial expressions possible in the face-to-face situation, but are not necessarily common in other parts of the country.

Expository writing, such as newspaper articles, essays, and editorials, are examples of more formal situations in which more complete sentences and precise word choices are necessary. In this kind of writing one cannot rely on nonverbal clauses to help the reader understand the message. In formal writing, localisms are generally avoided; the rare ones used for special effect are usually put in quotation marks.

When changing from one situation to another, be prepared to change the sentence structure and vocabulary used. This requires practice and begins with an awareness of the differences between the requirements of various situations. The diagram below will help display the differences in situations which are a matter of degree of completeness and formality.

informal   formal

incomplete sentences commonly expected	incomplete sentences accepted for effect	incomplete sentences accepted in dialogue	incomplete sentences rarely accepted
Conversation	*Advertising*	*Fiction*	*Expository Writing*
complete sentences not always expected	complete sentences accepted but not always required	complete sentences expected except in dialogue	complete sentences required except in rare cases for special effects

Diagram reprinted from *Grammar Lives*, Ronald Shephard and John MacDonald, Evanston, Illinois: McDougal, Littell and Co., 1975, p. 120.

Editing and Revision. Very few authors are capable of producing a finished piece of writing without revision; it is a fundamental part of the writing process. Revision involves more than simply correcting mistakes. Rather it is a systematic rethinking and reworking of the entire written effort to achieve three goals:

1. Economy — written work which fulfills a unified and limited purpose.

2. Clarity — written development which leads the reader from beginning to end, not letting him lose his way.

3. Impact — the proportion of emphasis that events, ideas, and descriptions must have in a written piece.

Revision requires a writer to be analytical and, at times, "cold blooded." He must be capable of "slashing his work to ribbons," or rewriting that preciously phrased passage, or of discarding what at the time seemed most effective.

In revising ask the following questions:

1. What is my ultimate purpose: my thesis statement, my topic sentence?

2. Can I accomplish this purpose within the limitation on length set for this piece?

3. Is the development of what I have written internally coherent?

4. What is the ultimate effect of my written work; have I given the reader the full impact of my most significant ideas?

5. Is my conclusion shallow and inconclusive, or does it leave the reader with a memorable thought centering on my ultimate purpose?

Revision is the key to truly good writing.

Expository Paragraph. Most student writing is an attempt to *explain*: answers to essay test questions, class reports, term papers, or lab experiments. This type of writing, called exposition (See also *Types of Writing*), calls for careful planning and organization because its primary purpose is to help the reader see the subject as the writer sees it; to see the reasons why a process works as it does; or why the writer feels as he does about a particular subject. Expository writing attempts to "reason out" an idea for a reader, "expose" the reasoning sequence, just as though the reader were thinking through the main idea himself.

Unity and Coherence. Because of the need for careful organization and complete development of an idea, the expository paragraph, probably the most useful unit of composition, operates on the following principles:

1. Unity — "Oneness"; that is, every sentence in the paragraph must pertain to a single idea established in the opening sentence of the paragraph called the *topic sentence.*

2. Coherence — "Flow"; that is, every sentence must link up naturally with the sentence following it in the paragraph.

In writing the paragraph, three devices are used to achieve these goals: the topic sentence, an outline support structure, and transition.

Topic Sentence. The topic sentence, is the first sentence in the paragraph, and must include a subject, limited so that it may be developed completely in about eight to twelve good sentences. In addition, the topic sentence must also include wording which tells specifically *what is to be proved* about the limited subject.

Controlling Idea. The wording, which makes up the predicate portion of the topic sentence (the part including the verb and anything to the right of the verb), is called the *controlling idea*, for it *controls* what can be said about the subject within the paragraph. For example, in the topic sentence:

Controlling Idea
Weather *has a definite effect on a person's mood.*

Weather is the subject to be discussed in the paragraph, but only information proving that weather *has a definite effect on a person's mood* can be used in the paragraph. All other material concerning weather or any other subject must be excluded. Likewise, in the topic sentence:

Controlling Idea
Membership in the National Honor Society *should be based on the difficulty of the courses a student takes.*

The subject to be discussed is *membership in the National Honor Society*, and the writer must *prove* that such membership should be based on the difficulty of courses a prospective member takes.

Note: Avoid topic sentences which are vague, or obvious, or which depend on judgment terms indicating individual preference such as "enjoyable" or "exciting."

Examples: Cooking and baking can really be *fun*.
Water skiing is an *enjoyable* sport.
Driving fast is *dangerous*.

Major and Minor Supports. Another device to insure unity and coherence within the paragraph is really a simple, two-stage outline which is used to determine what information should be included in the paragraph and to organize all the sentences following the topic sentence into an explanation or proof of the controlling idea. For example, the proof for the topic sentence:

Controlling Idea
Oil spills *have a harmful effect on all forms of life.*

may be outlined as follows:

Major Support	I.	The millions of gallons of oil spilled each year destroy marine wildlife.
Minor Support	A.	Many species of fish are killed by "oil poisoning."
Minor Support	B.	Also affected are the tiny animals which larger fish feed on, reducing their food supply.
Major Support	II.	The destruction of these fish reduces man's food supply.
Minor Support	A.	For example, man depends on fish for a significant part of his protein intake.
Minor Support	B.	Without this source of protein, man might use up all other available sources, thus producing harmful effects on his diet.
Major Support	III.	Finally, the spilled oil creates critical chemical imbalances supporting various life functions.
Minor Support	A.	The spilled oil causes breakdowns in oxygen vital to maintaining a balanced food chain.
Minor Support	B.	The oil also breaks down salt groups which must remain stable if stable eco-systems are to be maintained.

Within this outline, the major supporting statements (the Roman numerals I, II, and III) act as definite and direct explanations of the controlling idea. Note that every major support links directly back to the controlling idea simply by inserting the word "because" between the topic sentence and the major support:

Oil spills have a harmful effect on all forms of life

"because"

I. The millions of gallons of oil spilled each year destroy marine wildlife.

"and because"

II. The destruction of these fish reduces man's food supply.

"and because"

III. The spilled oil creates critical chemical imbalances supporting life functions.

Likewise, within the outline, the minor supporting statements (the capital A and B) act as specific illustrations, examples, or details which explain and prove the major support to which they are linked and, therefore, also prove the controlling idea. Note that these minor supports also link to their major statements simply by inserting the word "because" between them:

I. The spilled oil creates critical chemical imbalances supporting the various life functions.

"because"

A. The spilled oil causes breakdown in oxygen vital to maintaining a balanced food chain.

"and because"

B. The oil also breaks down salt groups which must remain stable if stable eco-systems are to be maintained.

Transition. Another device used to achieve coherence, a smooth "flow" from one sentence to the next within the paragraph, is transition. The logical order or reasoning pattern of the major and minor supports just discussed is very important in explaining ideas, but showing the connections between these statements is equally important. This connection or transition between sentences is accomplished in these ways:

1. By connecting words or phrases which show relationships between ideas.

Transition Word
Example: I believe Bill is right. *However,* several people have disagreed with him.

Note: Common transition words and the relationships they show include:

Addition: *and, also, in addition, furthermore, moreover*
Contrast: *but, yet, however, still, although, though, nevertheless, on the other hand*
Time: *first, second, next, then, finally, later, when, after, before, until, a few days later, at the same time*
Position: *behind, here, there, around, next to, to the right of, down, up, close to*
Cause and Result: *therefore, thus, as a result, consequently*
Manner or Method: *thus, for example, similarly, in this way*
Condition: *if, unless, until*

2. By repeating key words or synonyms for key words throughout the paragraph. These key words are usually the subject and the controlling idea.

Example: The girls learned how to play *bridge.*
They found the *game* very interesting, and decided to play *bridge* often.

Note: *Game* is a synonym for *bridge* and refers back to that key term, thus tying the two sentences together.

3. By using pronoun reference.

                                                           Pronoun

Example: Bill and Jim arrived late for school. However, *they* had good
                 Pronoun
        reason for *their* tardiness.

Note: *They* and *their* refer back to *Bill and Jim* in the first sentence and
therefore tie the two sentences together.

The following paragraph, was written by a student. It illustrates the paragraph
writing techniques listed previously:

	Subject
Topic Sentence:	A knowledge of regional or state road maps *can be*

                                 Controlling Idea
                       very helpful to a driver in three basic ways.

                     Transition   Key Term
Major Support: I.   *First,* when planning a trip, the *driver* with a *knowl-*
                     Key Term
               edge of maps can choose a specific route to his desti-
               nation depending on how he wishes to travel.

                  A.   For fast and safe travel he may select the multi-
                        lane highways, designated as such on the map.

                     Transition
                  B.   *On the other hand,* if time is available, he may
                        choose a scenic route and view some points of
                                     Pronoun Reference
                        interest along the way. In both of *these* cases,
                            Key Term
                        if the person driving *knows how to read a map,*
                        with little trouble, he can find the route he
                        wishes to take.

                     Transition
Major Support: II.   *Second,* when he is traveling in an unfamiliar region,
                     Key Term
               the *driver* can use maps to avoid getting lost.

                     Transition
                  A.   *For instance,* all maps show major roads in a
                        particular area, and most maps show minor
                        roads, making it difficult for a driver with a
                              Key Term
                        knowledge of road maps to lose his way.

Transition

B. *And* although not every little town is indicated, most small and medium size towns are marked
Key Term
on the maps so that the *driver* may still be able to find his way by checking for various cities and towns along the route.

Transition   Key Term

Major Support: III. *Finally*, a *driver* may use the map inserts, "points of interest" guide, and other information charts contained in most maps to modify his journey as circumstances require.

A. Since a driver may be confused by the maze of street detours and other unforeseen obstacles in large cities, metropolitan map inserts may provide enough information to alter his route as he proceeds.

Transition

B. *Also*, the guides often show some of the more important points of interest that the driver may wish to visit in a particular region if he finds himself with additional time to do so.

Parallel Structure. Writing should be consistent. Phrases in a series of two or more should be similarly worded.

Example: Wrong: Going hiking, to bicycle, and to camp are my favorite summer activities.
Right: Hiking, bicycling, and camping are my favorite summer activities.

Tense of verbs must be consistent.

Example: Wrong: I went to work early, and I see my boss arrive.
Right: I went to work early, and I saw my boss arrive.

Ideas in a sentence that are equally important should be expressed in parallel (or similar) grammatical forms:

Examples: Not parallel: Entering the room, Karen began to tap her toes, wave her hands, and jumping to the music.
Parallel: Entering the room, Karen began tapping her toes, waving her hands, and jumping to the music.

61

Not parallel:	Swimming, jogging, and even a walk are good forms of exercise.
Parallel:	Swimming, jogging, and even walking are good forms of exercise.

Good parallel structure helps the reader see the logic of the writer's ideas and makes the writing flow smoothly.

Example: To succeed you need to analyze the problem, suggest solutions, and choose the most practical alternative.

See also *Sentence Structures* and *Sentence Patterns.*

Literary Terms. In literature, some terms are often used to analyze and discuss the ways in which authors use words. This is a short list of some of the more frequently used terms. Since space is limited in this handbook, you should refer to a dictionary or handbook of literary terms for the many not on this list.

Allegory: Extended metaphor in which characters, objects, incidents, and descriptions carry one or more fully developed meanings in addition to the apparent literal one.

Alliteration: The repetition of initial consonant sounds in a phrase or line of speech or writing. Example: wailing in the winter wind.

Antagonist: The chief rival or opponent of the protagonist.

Anthology: A collection of literary pieces, such as poems, short stories, or plays, usually suggesting a theme.

Autobiography: The recollections of a person's life written by himself.

Biography: The story of a person's life written by another person.

Characterization: The creation of imaginary persons in literature, often by imitating or describing actions, gestures, or speeches. There are three basic methods of characterization: (1) the direct presentation of the character through direct exposition, either in a single introduction or more often piece-meal throughout the work, illustrated by action; (2) the presentation of the character by his actions, with little or no outright comment by the author, so that the reader is expected to figure out the person through these actions; and, (3) the representation of the character's thoughts and feelings so that, with little or no comment by the author, the reader is able to figure out the character.

Climax: In the essay, short story, drama, or novel, the climax is the point of highest interest; at this point the reader responds with the greatest emotion. It also is the turning point in the action.

Comedy: A play, motion picture, or other work that is humorous in its theme and usually ends happily.

Conflict: The struggle which grows out of the clash of opposing forces in the plot, providing interest and suspense. This may be divided into four different kinds: (1) man may struggle against the forces of nature, as in Jack London's "To Build a Fire"; (2) he may struggle against another person, usually the antagonist, as in Stevenson's *Treasure Island*; (3) he may struggle against society as a force, as in Dickens' *Great Expectations*; or (4) two elements within him may struggle for mastery, as in Brutus in Shakespeare's *Julius Caesar*. It is seldom that a single, simple conflict is used in a plot. Usually a complex plot line uses two or more of these elements.

Connotation: The cluster of implications that words or phrases may carry with them, as distinguished from their literal meanings. These may be (1) private and personal, the result of individual experience, (2) group (national, linguistic, racial), or (3) general or universal, held by all or most people.

Context: The part of a written or spoken statement in which a specific word or passage occurs. It leads up to, follows, and often specifies the meaning of a particular expression.

Denotation: The specific, exact meaning of a word, separated from its emotional associations.

Denouement: The final unraveling of the plot in drama or fiction, the solution of the mystery, the explanation or outcome.

Dialogue: The conversation of two or more people as reproduced in writing.

Dramatic Structure: The plot of a drama compares with the tying and untying of a knot. It is the technical structure of a play which is sometimes represented as a pyramid, the rising slope suggesting the rising action or tying of the knot, the falling slope representing the untying, and the apex representing the climax. Traditionally there are five parts to dramatic structure: the introduction, rising action, climax, falling action, and catastrophe or conclusion.

Essay: Usually said to be a moderately brief prose discussion of a restricted topic.

Euphemism: A figure of speech in which an indirect, positive, optimistic, or cheerful statement is substituted for a direct one in an effort to avoid bluntness. Example: *passed away* instead of *died.*

Falling Action: The second half or resolution of a dramatic plot. It follows the climax and culminates in the catastrophe.

Farce: A Latin word meaning "to stuff" which originally referred to the addition of comic jokes and gags to the original plot until the laughter and humor became more important than the plot. Today it is generally used to describe a situation that is ludicrous, an empty show, or mockery.

Foreshadowing: Provides a hint of what is to occur later in a literary work.

Hyperbole: Extravagant exaggeration used as a figure of speech. Example: My cat weighs a ton.

Irony: A figure of speech in which the actual intent is expressed in words which carry the opposite meaning. Antony's insistence in his funeral oration in *Julius Ceasar* that "Brutus is an honorable man" is an example.

Malapropism: Inappropriate use of one word for another because of some similarity between them. Example: baked elastic, a crop irritation system, or a hungry allegory on the banks of the Nile.

Metaphor: A figure of speech in which a word denoting one subject or idea is used in place of another to suggest a likeness between them. Example: All the world's a stage.

Onomatopoeia: The use of a word that sounds like what it refers to. Example: The bees buzz.

Novel: A fictitious prose narrative of considerable length portraying characters, actions, and scenes.

Personification: A figure of speech which endows animals, ideas, abstractions, and inanimate objects with human action, form, character, or personality. Example: Flowers danced in the breeze.

Plot: The series of planned and interrelated actions which move through conflict and characterization to a climax and resolution. The action of the narrative.

Point of View: The position from which the reader is presented with the story. It is the author's vantage point from which he presents the action. If the author serves as an all-knowing maker, not restricted to time, place, or character and free to move or comment at will, the point of view is usually called omniscient. At the other extreme, the story may be told by a character within the story as he saw or experienced it. This is usually called a first person point of view. The author may tell a story in the third person and yet present it as it is seen and understood by a single character, restricting information to what that character sees, hears, feels, and thinks; such a point of view is called third person limited.

Protagonist: The main character of a piece of writing with whom the reader or viewer is led to identify.

Rising Action: The part of a dramatic plot which has to do with the complication of the action. It is the movement of the conflict to the climax.

Setting: The physical background against which the action of the plot takes place. The time and location of a piece of literature.

Satire: Writing which attempts to use humor and wit to improve human institutions or humanity.

64

Simile: A figure of speech which directly compares two objects. It often is introduced by the words *like* or *as.* Example: She is *like* a playful kitten.

Style: The manner of writing which best expresses the idea and the individuality of the author. It is the way in which a writer adapts language to his ideas in seeking his own unique and effective means of expression.

Synecdoche: A form of metaphor in which a part stands for the whole (or in which the whole stands for a part). Example: the use of "wheels" to refer to an automobile.

Theme: The central or dominating idea of a piece of literature.

Tragedy: A drama in prose or verse which recounts an important series of events in a person's life which leads to a catastrophe.

Misused Words. The following pairs of words are often used interchangeably with a resulting confusion of meaning. Be sure that you know the difference between them. When in doubt, check a dictionary.

a, an	emigrate, immigrate
able, capable	export, import
accept, except	formerly, formally
adapt, adopt	good, well
affect, effect	have, of
all right, (alright)	imply, infer
all together, altogether	lay, lie
allusion, illusion, delusion	learn, teach
(alot), a lot, allot	leave, let
already, all ready	lend, loan
amount, number	like, as
awful, awfully	loose, lose
bad, badly	me, myself
because, that	morale, moral
beside, besides	payed, paid
between, among	precede, proceed
breath, breathe	principal, principle
bring, take	raise, rise
by, at, in	read, read, red
by, for	real, really
by, near	rear, raise
can, may	set, sit
certain, sure(ly)	their, there, they're
continuous, continual	them, those
desert, dessert, desert	wait on, wait for

Redundancy. Redundancy is the use of unnecessary words. Sentences should be concise. Those which are wordy are poor sentences that should be revised. For clarity and economy remove unnecessary words and needlessly complicated expressions from your writing. Sometimes words merely repeat the sense of other words, as in "the modern girl *of today.*" Sometimes they modify an idea already modified, as in "*true* facts" or "visible *to the eye.*" Both are errors of redundancy.

Here are sentences containing redundancies (in brackets) that should be omitted:

He died at the age of eighty [years old].
The new field house is extremely large [in size].
The nasturtiums, mostly a bright orange [in color], were my favorites [that I liked best].
We shall combine the three chapters [into one].
[Any and] all of the birds can be eaten for dinner.
There were four [different] kinds of fish on the menu.
The [end] result was that we had several keys.
[The person who is] the driver should keep her eyes on the road.

Do not use inflated, roundabout expressions when simpler, more direct statements will do.

Examples: *Wordy:* It was the month of June that the flu became a problem of great seriousness.
More direct: In June, the flu became a serious problem.

Wordy: Whenever it happens to rain, my corner always floods the streets full of water.
More direct: Whenever it rains, my corner is flooded.

Some students have the mistaken idea that inflated phrases make their writing sound more authoritative. Others, anxious to meet the assigned length without doing the necessary thinking or research, use roundabout expressions to make their writing longer. The result is poor writing that sounds pompous and is confusing in its wordiness. Make every word pull its share of the load of meaning and ideas.

Types of Writing. While the same basic principles apply to most writing, different kinds of writing have purposes and problems of their own. Here are four familiar types: exposition, description, narration, and argumentation.

Exposition. Exposition is *explanation* of a subject. Its purpose is to make the reader understand. It tells what a thing is, how it functions, how its parts are related to each other, or how it is related to other things. An article setting forth the structure of the government of the United States, or the germ theory of diseases would be expository in that it would convey an accurate and coherent explanation of these subjects.

Expository writing addresses itself to the intellect; it does not try to move or influence, and it does not try to impress, except with the truth. A large majority of the lectures given in high school and college are expository in that they present information in an organized way. The simple directions you give people about doing things or going places are elementary examples of exposition.

Because it is used to transmit knowledge by explanation, exposition is probably the most widely used of all forms of writing. School term papers, school textbooks, car manuals, cookbooks, reference books, informational articles in magazines, and business reports, are all expository in technique and purpose.

Description. The primary purpose of most description is to make the reader *see* things or perceive the special quality of them. It focuses upon the appearance of an object while exposition focuses upon the nature of it.

The nature writer, for example, makes us share in the sights and sounds of the natural world in which we live. An account of travel makes us visualize objects, people, and scenes. Imagination is important in descriptive writing. Unlike exposition, the personal reactions and feelings of the writer color what he describes.

Narration. This kind of writing tells what is popularly recognized as a "story." Like description, narration is concerned with evoking pictures in time. Narration is probably the most elementary and ancient form of writing.

Argumentation. This kind of writing is distinguished from the other three forms in that its function is to prove. Its methods of proof have been reduced to a science known as logic, whereby one can say with some certainty whether a given statement has been made good by the evidence offered in support of it. Argumentation, usually concerned with matters of policy, includes the formal argument used in debates in courts of law, and in much reflective and philosophical writing.

Usage. The degree of formality of English can generally be arranged along a continuum (See also *Dialect*.) with informal conversation at one end and formal exposition at the other. In discussing writing the ends and center of this continuum are often labeled nonstandard, informal, and formal. While these are not rigid categories, the terms can provide a useful description of the differences of style and tone available to the writer. The following sections describe the three levels of English usage, formal English, informal English, and nonstandard English; and some common problems of language usage, cliche', shoptalk, slang, trite expressions, and verb-adverb combinations.

Formal English. Formal English is used by educated people on formal occasions. Graduation speeches, scientific reports, legal papers, and business reports as well as essays, some fiction, biography, and poetry are all types of formal writing. While good formal writing involves careful word choices and sentence construction, that does not mean that it is necessarily heavy and stiff. It is appropriate when precision and accuracy are important.

Informal English. Informal English lies between the two extremes of formal and nonstandard English and encompasses the majority of our speaking and writing. It is the most frequently used in classroom and business situations. It could be defined as the speech of educated people tidied up to please the reader. This is the most important level for you to have a command of for most occasions in your life.

Nonstandard English. Nonstandard English is used by people of little formal education, or whose education has not changed their speech and writing. It is most often used by persons who rarely write except for personal matters. It is marked by frequent use of slang and nonstandard pronunciation. It is not necessarily "bad" English. It is simply one kind of English — and serves a great many people perfectly well. But educated people, whose work and personal interests usually involve constant use of language, who are often reading, writing, and talking about complex matters, who have to express things exactly and in a way that meets the approval of other educated people, find that nonstandard English just will not do the job. They avoid it.

Cliche.́ An expression that has been used so often that it has become commonplace and stale is called a cliche ́and is a common problem.

Examples: clean as a whistle, selling like hotcakes, knee-high to a grasshopper, few and far between.

See also *Trite Expressions.*

Shoptalk. Shoptalk is the special vocabulary used by people in their occupations but is a problem in usage. Electricians deal with *ohms, anodes*, and *amps.* Hockey players talk about *icing, face-offs*, and *hat tricks..* Some shoptalk terms have been adopted into the general vocabulary. Space flights and lunar landings have introduced such space shoptalk as *A-OK, splash down, lunar module*, and *countdown.* Generally, shoptalk is not appropriate for speaking or writing that is intended for a general, non-specialist audience.

Slang. Novelty, the chief attraction of slang, quickly wears off after its hundreds of repetitions, and the expressions lose their freshness and become cliche's. Much slang is too vague to give more than a general impression of approval or disapproval. Words like *neat, groovy, harsh,* and *crummy* are slang of this kind and add little to style or meaning. While it is sometimes used in informal writing, particularly dialogue or narrative, it is inappropriate in most composition situations and should be avoided in formal speech or writing.

Trite Expressions. Trite expressions are figures of speech that through constant overuse have lost their original effectiveness. They may be old, shopworn expressions such as *take a dim view* or *dyed in the wool*; or they may be currently popular such as *do your own thing.* They should be avoided.

Verb—Adverb Combinations. In the sentence "The dictator put down the rebellion," the word *down* (although technically an adverb) in meaning is part of the verb. *Put* literally means "place," but the combination *put down* means "suppress"; it has nothing to do with "placing". These verb-adverb combinations, two-part verbs that have a meaning different from the literal meaning of each word, are frequent in informal English. Formal English is likely to prefer single words: *investigate* for *look into, conclude* for *wrap up.* See also *Idiom.*

Part III: Special Composition Forms

Book or Article Review. A critical discussion of a book or article, especially a newly published one, is called a review. Such a review usually contains some indication of the contents of the book or article and some comment on the author's purpose, style, and accomplishment.

Common organization for an article review is as follows:

Article Title _____

I.   In one sentence state the *main idea* discussed in this article. Depending on whether the article is written to analyze a problem or just to offer information on a particular subject, the main idea may be either a *problem to be solved* or *a topic of interest or concern to people.*

II. If the article analyzes a problem, list the *causes of the problem* or, if it is an informational article, list the *reasons why the subject is of interest or concern.*

III. List *possible solutions* or *recommendations* offered in the article.

IV. In 5-7 sentences discuss the importance of this topic. If possible, use specific examples from the article to support your answer.

Note: In some cases you might argue that the topic is not of importance; if so explain carefully.

Common organization for a book review is as follows:

In Place of a Title:

Use the bibliographic data for your book: author, title, city of publication, publisher, year of publication (original date) and number of pages. The following is an example:

Payne, Lucile Vaughan. *The Lively Art of Writing.* Chicago: Follett Publishing Co., 1965, 192 pages.

First Paragraph: Introduction

In three to five carefully worded sentences, explain why the author wrote the book. What ideas and attitudes was he trying to express?

Include the name of the book (underlined), the author, and the literary category it belongs to (historical, narrative, documentary, collection of essays, biography, autobiography, novel, etc.).

Second Paragraph: A Short Summary

Describe the subjects covered in the book. Include enough information to convince your teacher you have read the book but not so much as to bore him/her.

Establish the time and place of the events.

Third Paragraph: Evaluation of the Book

Explain how the book is organized (chapters, sub-books, letters, journal or diary entries, collection of essays, etc.). Was the organization helpful or confusing? Why?

Was the vocabulary within your reach? If necessary, explain or give examples to support your answer.

Do you think there are people who would benefit from reading this book? Who? What benefit? Why do you say so?

Did you benefit from it? How?

Why or why not is the book interesting to high school students?

Letter Writing. Of all the forms of writing, a letter makes the most direct contact with its reader. A good letter provides a format for the writer to talk directly to the reader. Usually a letter is designed to be read by a specific individual; its organization should be clear, its sentences short, and its words well chosen.

In letter writing certain customary forms should be observed whether the letter is a business or personal letter. The following sections contain examples of common letter and envelope forms:

Business Letters. The business letter usually has six parts. Note their placement and punctuation:

Heading	101 Oak Street Polonia, WI 50000 May 6, 1979
Inside Address	Mr. Elwood Black Stevens Point Daily Bugle 604 N. Second Street Stevens Point, WI 54481
Salutation	Dear Mr. Black:
Body	Please send me the brochure on "Home Smoke Alarms" which was offered in your column in the Daily Bugle of May 4. I am enclosing 50 cents in coin to cover mailing and handling costs.
Closing	Yours truly,
Signature	*George Hermann* George Hermann

Another frequently used business form is the block form. Here is an example:

Heading	685 Main Street Plover, Wisconsin 54467 January 18, 1979
Inside Address	Mr. John Jacoby Metaphor Knitting Mill 181 Purl Road Argyle, Wisconsin 42301
Salutation	Dear Mr. Jacoby:
Body	Last month I ordered one Alpine Girl sweater, size 38, from your company. I enclosed my check for $18.75. This morning I received three pairs of Valley Boy earmuffs. I am sending them back to be exchanged for the sweater. I have included your shipping invoice. Thank you for correcting this error.
Closing	Sincerely,
Signature	*Betty Farwell* (Ms.) Betty Farwell
Reference, enclosure or carbon copy	Enclosure

If the person addressed has a title, it is included inside after his name. It may be put on a separate line below the name. (Most dictionaries have a section telling how to address governors, senators, bishops, and so on.) If it is not directed to a particular person, the inside address consists of three lines.

Mr. Farley N. Welwood   Women Ski Flyers, Inc.
Director of Admissions   Box 1984
Slurry College   Iola, WI 54404
Baird, Colorado 23402

If the letter is not addressed to a particular person, use one of the following salutations:

Dear Sir: Dear Madam:
Gentlemen: Ladies:

Use one of three closings to end the letter:

Very truly yours,   Sincerely,   Cordially yours,

While a man does not write the title Mr. before his signature, a woman may write Miss or Ms. in parentheses before her name or add her married name below her signature to indicate how the reply should be addressed.

Very truly yours,   Cordially yours,

(Ms.) Joan Adamski   *Ruth J. Atwell*

                            (Mrs. Henry A. Atwell)

Envelope Address. The envelope makes use of ZIP codes and state abbreviations. (See also *Zip Code Abbreviations of State Names.*)

Example:

Carol Kulas
211 Howe Road, Apt. 115
Stevens Point, WI 54481

Mr. J. G. Wood, Manager
Sugarhill Farm
Rural Route 1, Box 48
Junction City, WI 54443

Since a business letter is usually written on 8½ x 11 inch paper, it is generally folded in one of two ways, depending on the size of the envelope.

For a long envelope —

For a short envelope —

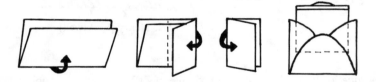

Personal Letters. Personal correspondence can be done in varying degrees of formality or informality depending on the person addressed and the occasion. While most personal letters are written to exchange news and ideas, occasionally a letter or note is needed for one specific purpose — a thank you, an invitation, a reply to an invitation, a congratulation, or an expression of sympathy. This letter is generally brief, seldom more than a paragraph or two.

Personal letters usually have five parts.

Heading

> 3345 Howell St.
> Plover, WI 54467
> January 3, 1979

Salutation

> Dear Mrs. Harding,

Body

> Your gift of a dozen live lobsters in a special "clambake kit" was easily the most memorable Christmas gift our family ever received. By the time we recaptured them, bandaged Priscilla's thumb, and retrieved the cat from the Christmas tree, we were all anticipating their appearance on the table (especially Mother). Your thoughtfulness will be long remembered by our entire family.

Closing

> Cordially,

Signature

> Samuel Splinter

Manuscript Form. Any written paragraph or report should be completed according to the following guidelines, unless otherwise specified.

1. Write on one side of standard size white paper (8½ x 11 inches). If you type, use standard size (8½ x 11 inch) white typing paper. Double space and use only one side of the paper.

2. Use blue, black, or blue-black ink or typewriter ribbon.

3. Put your name, the course title and period, teacher's name, and date in order, one below the other, in the upper right-hand corner of the first page. Write only your name on the following pages.

4. Number all pages except the first. Paperclip or staple multiple pages; do not "dog-ear" or fold to hold them together.

5. Leave the following margins: left — 1½", bottom — 1", right — 1".

6. Place the title in the center of the first line of a ruled page, and skip a line between the title and the beginning of the first paragraph. Do not underline the title; when typing, the title of the composition is to be placed about two inches below the top of the page and centered. Do not enclose the title in quotation marks.

7. Indent the first line of each paragraph one inch (or five spaces). Skip a space between paragraphs only when typing.

8. Proofread your work carefully. A few minutes of reading your paper over will pay off.

9. Papers should be neat. If a mistake is made, draw one line through the mistake and continue the paper. Do not make insertions between lines and afterthought additions in the margins. If changes must be made on the final copy, make them neatly or rewrite the entire page.

	Student's Name Course Name, Period Teacher's Name Date Title (on first line) Skip a line (or 2 spaces) Indent one inch (or five spaces) to begin the first paragraph.	
----1½"----		----1½"----

Reference Work. The research paper is a summary of what others have written on a given subject. Therefore, in writing a paper, you are not so much adding to the available information on a subject as making use of information that is already known. However, you can be original in the *selection* and *organization* of the material which you have researched and in the *conclusions* which you arrive at as a result of the research.

Because the research paper is intended to provide information for a reader in a relatively simple and direct manner, certain basic writing techniques are used universally, particularly in footnoting and bibliography work, so that your research can easily be read and understood even by the casual reader. Therefore, even though some of the "rules" associated with footnoting and bibliography may seem arbitrary and even "picky," these rules are necessary to make detailed reference information understandable.

The notation and organization of scientific papers differ from this format and are discussed in *Science Reports and Papers*.

Common Reference Sources. To begin a research paper, you will need to make use of library materials which can provide important information. Here is a list of sources that have been found particularly useful.

1. Dictionary — meanings, sources, pronunciations of words.
2. Encyclopedia — short articles on most subjects.
3. *Roget's Thesaurus* — lists many synonyms for words.
4. *Reader's Guide to Periodical Literature* — lists magazine articles by subject.
5. *World Almanac* and *Information Please Almanac* — up-to-date facts and figures on thousands of subjects.
6. *Contemporary Authors* — biographies, addresses, and publications; lists of current writers.
7. *Robert's Rules of Order* — correct procedures for running democratic meetings.
8. *Current Biography* — famous living people, their life stories and achievements.
9. *Bartlett's Familiar Quotations* — collection of famous quotations.
10. Granger's *Index to Poetry* — titles, first lines, and authors of poems.
11. *Statistical Abstract of the United States* — facts and figures on government programs, geography, population, etc.
12. *Statesman's Yearbook* — government, population, monetary systems, agriculture, industry of all countries in the world.
13. *Who's Who* — a series of books giving capsule biographies of famous people.
14. *Famous First Facts* — lists the first time an event has occurred, when, and where.

Research Tips. Taking good notes is one of the most important study skills and fundamental to writing the research paper. Follow these tips and remember to write down the *important facts*, not every scrap of information.

1. Pay full attention.

2. Watch for word signals indicating the thought relationships in your reading. There are four types:
   a. Some words show *main points.*
      Examples: first, second, next
   b. Some words show *additional information* will be given.
      Examples: also, and, in addition
   c. Some words show *opposites* or *different ideas.*
      Examples: but, however, on the other hand
   d. Some words point toward *conclusion* (summary).
      Examples: thus, therefore, in conclusion, so

3. Take notes in your *own* words except for information which you will want to give in a direct quotation within your paper.

4. Review what you've written down soon after the note-taking. If it doesn't make sense, perhaps you will remember how to correct it.

5. Write down only new, main ideas — not what you already know.

6. Be precise.

7. Record the *exact source* of your notes carefully and completely, before you put the source away. See also *Footnotes* and *Bibliography* in this section.

Note Taking. Although you may be tempted to jot down research notes in notebooks or on random scraps of paper in hopes of saving time, one of the most practical and time saving methods of collecting information for your paper involves the following steps.

1. Write your notes on 4x6 inch cards so that notes may be set in the order of your outline and reorganized if changes in the outline become necessary. (3x5 inch cards are generally too small)

2. Place information concerning only *one outline heading* (slug) and *one reference source* on a card.

3. Label the note card by:
   A. Putting the *outline heading* in the upper left hand corner identifying the information recorded on the card.
   B. Putting the *author's name* and *an abbreviation of the title* of the reference source in the upper right hand corner. (If you are numbering or coding your bibliography cards, simply record the number of the call letter of the bibliography card that identifies this source).

4. Write in the left margin the pages where the material was found in the reference source.

5. Take notes carefully, remembering that notes may be used to summarize, paraphrase, or quote directly. However, be sure that material is paraphrased accurately and quoted precisely.

6. If notes are continued on another card, repeat the heading on each succeeding card and number the cards in sequence.

7. Arrange cards in order according to your outline and rearrange only when adjustments in the outline are made.

Examples of the above follow:

Outline Segment

> I. Definitions of Love
>   A. Greek Words for Love
>   B. Contemporary interpretations of the word love

Note Card

Slug

Summary

Direct Quotation (note the Quotation marks)

> *Love: Greek Definitions*   Short, *Sex, Love*
>
> 43-44 Five Greek definitions:
>   1. Sensual Love — Sexual desire (epithymia)
>   2. Yearning for unity — unity with something attractive (eros)
>   3. Brotherly love — love shared with friends (philia)
>   4. Family affection — love shared with parents and children (storge)
>   5. Self-giving love — devotion to others regardless of merit (agape)
>
> 44   "Clearly, each of these five words used by the Greeks has its own distinct meaning. Each is quite different from all the rest."

Bibliography* Card

Author

Title

City of publication, Publisher, Copyright Date, Page Numbers

> Short, Ray E.
>
> *Sex, Love or Infatuation: How Can I Really Know?*
>
> Minneapolis, Augsburg Publishing House, 1978, pp. 38-51.

*Make sure that all information needed to complete the bibliography and footnotes included in the research paper is recorded on the bibliography card.

Outlining. During note-taking develop an outline to organize your paper. The following is one suggested form for outlining.

Popular Cat Breeds	title
I. Angora	main idea
A. Appearance	major support
1. Coat	minor support
a. Silky, fine, and long	details
b. Ruff on neck and bushy tail	
2. Body structure	minor support
a. Long body	details
b. Pointed head	
i. Long ears	
ii. Long nose	
B. History	major support
1. Originated in Ankara, Turkey	minor support
2. Imported to U.S. in eighteenth century	minor support
II. Siamese	second main idea
A. Appearance	major support
1. Coat	minor support
a. Short and sleek	details
b. Darker on legs, face, and tail	
2. Body Structure	minor support
a. Long, slender body	details
b. Wedge-shaped head	
B. History	major support
1. Originated in Thailand	minor support
2. Imported to U.S., late nineteenth century	minor support

See also *Expository Paragraph* for information on how the parts of an outline should fit together.

Footnotes. Whenever ideas are taken from the writings of others, credit must be given to those from whom the information is gained. Courtesy toward your sources and the integrity of your own work demand this be done since your readers will judge the quality of your work in terms of the sources that you use in putting your paper together. Footnotes are also very helpful since they give the reader necessary information on your sources so that he can turn directly to them for more material on the subject. Informational footnotes may also be used to explain, illustrate, or evaluate statements made in the main text of the paper.

Footnotes are used:

1. To give the source of a direct quotation.

2. To give credit for another writer's ideas even though they are expressed in your own words.

3. To give the source of diagrams, tables, charts, definitions, or illustrations.

Footnote directions:

1. A direct quotation consisting of less than five lines of text should be enclosed in quotation marks and combined smoothly into your own sentence.

2. A quotation of more than five lines of text should be handled as follows:

   a. Double-space above and below the quotation.
   b. Single-space the quoted material.
   c. Indent material an additional half-inch within the margins on both sides.
   d. *Do not* use quotation marks.

3. Number footnotes consecutively throughout the paper.

4. Place the number slightly above the line at the end of the last sentence to be footnoted. No period follows the number.

5. Footnotes may be typed at the bottom of each page, placing the number in front of and above the footnote line. Indent the first line of each footnote and start the second line even with the left margin. Footnotes may also be listed on a separate page between the appendices (if any) and the bibliography.

6. Single-space footnotes which require more than one line.

7. Leave a one-line space between footnotes on the same page.

Example of footnoted text:

According to McNally and Florescu, "The American horror film became popular because of the almost simultaneous release of two remarkable creatures: Dracula the vampire (1931) and Dr. Frankenstein's monster (1932)."[1] They drew a parallel between the forces in society that made these films popular and the economic history of the time.

It is interesting to speculate on whether there is any correlation between the popularity of these creatures and the period in which they were released — the Great Depression. The optimistic Dr. Frankenstein created a monster which ultimately destroyed him, just as many optimistic investors created a market situation which in 1929 destroyed them.[2]

Examples of footnotes: (See also *Science Reports and Papers.*)

1. The first time a source is given:

A book:

[1]Thomas Elliot Berry, *The Most Common Mistakes in English Usage* (New York, McGraw-Hill, 1971), p. 22.

A book with no author's name listed:

[2]*Webster's Biographical Dictionary* (Springfield, Mass., G.C. Merriam Co., 1971), p. 20.

A book that is edited:

[3]Thomas Wolfe, "The Story of a Novel," in *The Thomas Wolfe Reader*, ed. by C. Hugh Holman (New York, Charles Scribner's Sons, 1962), pp. 11-50.

An anthology:

[4]Robert Frost, "Mending Wall," in *Modern American Poetry*, ed. by Louis Untermeyer (New York, Harcourt Brace, Inc., 1958), p. 180.

An encyclopedia article:

[5]"Tides," *Encyclopedia Britannica* (1962 ed.), XXII, 201.

A signed magazine article:

[6]Bill Johnson, "Typing in the Public Schools," *American Education Journal*, 118 (March, 1977), p. 81.

An unsigned magazine article:

[7]"Unique Camera Records," *American Photography*, 21 (July 18, 1970), p. 208.

A signed news story:

[8]Henry Giniger, "France Protests War," *The New York Times* (May 10, 1973), p. 9.

An unsigned news story:

[9]"Peace in our Time," *The Milwaukee Journal* (December 10, 1977), p. 10.

2. For a source which has been given in the footnote immediately preceding this footnote:

    [10]*Ibid.*, p. 21. (Give page number only if different from the one given in the preceding footnote.)

3. For a source by an author when only one work by that author has been used:

    [11]James, p. 80.

4. For a source by an author when more than one work by that author has been used:

    [12]James, *Goals*, p. 52. (Give a shortened version of the title: *The Goals of our Society.*)

5. For a source with no author's name which has been used before:

    [13]*Webster's Collegiate*, p. 281. (Give a shortened version of the title.)

6. For a magazine article which has been used before:

    [14]*Saturday Review*, p. 89. (If, however, more than one article is used from the same magazine, the footnote is given in full.)

84

Bibliography. The sources, the books, magazines, or encyclopedias you have used, are listed on a separate page at the end of your report. You must list the information in a very exact manner so the reader will be able to locate this information in any library.

1. Sources are alphabetized by the first word of the entries.

2. The sources are *not* numbered.

3. The first lines of each entry should be in a straight line down the page; the second line of each entry is indented five spaces and kept in a straight line.

4. Follow the order and punctuation as listed below for each of the different kinds of sources.

BIBLIOGRAPHY

Dalton, Dudley. "Changing L.I. Viewed Aloft," *New York Times*, Aug. 3, 1975 (Section I), p. 77.	*Newspaper article*
Deschin, Jacob. *Say It With Camera*. New York: Ziff-Davis, 1960.	*Book with one author*
Ellis, Joe and Peter Johnson. *Camera Techniques*. New York: Crowell, 1970.	*Book with two authors*
Halverson, Warner, photography instructor, Stevens Point Area Senior High School. Personal interview. Stevens Point, Wisconsin, April 20, 1979.	*Interview*
"Photography," *Encyclopedia Britannica*, 1962, XX, 480.	*Encyclopedia (unsigned article)*
Rothstein, Arthur. "Creative Color: Art Through Photography," *U.S. Camera and Travel*, 32:80-86, July 14, 1971.	*Magazine article (If no author is given, start with title of article)*
U.S. Department of Labor. Wages and Labor Standards Administration. *Photography Safety Standards*. Bulletin 314. Washington, D.C.: U.S. Government Printing Office, 1976.	*Document*

Note: It is suggested that the bibliography of your research paper should actually be prepared as you take notes for your paper. As you take notes on a particular source, record the following bibliographical information for that source on a separate 3x5 inch card.

1. The author's full name (last name first because your bibliography will be typed in alphabetical order).

2. The exact title (including article from magazine or newspaper).

3. The place of publication, publisher, and date of publication (volume number, month and year of publication, and page numbers of articles from magazines and newspapers.)

Set up this information on the 3x5 inch card exactly as you will type it in the bibliography of your research paper, including the correct punctuation. This will save you much time in preparing your footnotes and typing your bibliography. See also *Note Taking* for bibliography card sample.

Resume´and Job Application. Whether you are looking for part-time or full-time work you will probably face the need to write letters of job application and/or a resume´. Doing this well may make the difference in whether or not you are hired. Showing that you care enough about the job to do this well may make an employer think you will approach your work the same way.

Letter of Application.

A. Steps to follow

1. The Product: Decide what your strong points are
2. The Market: Find out who the buyers are and what appeals to them
3. The Contact: Write the application letter and get a personal interview

B. Five steps of application

1. Establish a point of contact.
   a. Physical appearance and arrangement of the letter
      1. Use good quality and white bond paper — usually plain, no letterhead
      2. Should be well paragraphed and attractively arranged
      3. Typewrite your application

b.   Statement of nature and purpose

Note: Your point of contact, the opening sentence, shows your purpose and tells where you, the applicant, learned of the position (newspaper ad, guidance counselor, individual who already works there, etc.), or mentions the name of the person who has suggested that you write. Your opening sentence should be followed by a specific statement that you are applying.

Example: In Thursday's *Daily Journal* I noticed your advertisement for a private secretary and correspondent. May I be considered for this position?

Or: I should like to apply for this position.

Or: Please consider me an applicant.

2.   Show how your education and training fit the requirements.
    a.   Give facts.
    b.   Establish a "you" attitude that will present a positive image.

Example: I am a graduate of SPASH where I took the three-year business course. During the past three years, I have been a student helper to Mr. Biser, the Industrial Arts teacher. My work for Mr. Biser included typing letters, filing, and record keeping. I can take dictation at 120 words a minute, transcribe my notes at 30 words a minute, and type straight copy at 80 words a minute. On my own responsibility I have handled much routine correspondence and have found this experience highly valuable in broadening my general business and secretarial ability. I have become thoroughly familiar with commercial and legal forms, including leases, deeds, and mortgages.

Note: Do not repeat lists in resume.

3.   Give your personal qualifications.
    a.   Explain why you feel confident you can be successful in the position.
    b.   Include touches of human interest — what you have experienced that everyone else has not.
    c.   Explain why you are interested in the employer's kind of business.
    d.   Tell about your activities in and out of school — those not listed in paragraph 2.

4.   Give references.
    a.   Give at least three
    b.   Correct and exact addresses   } information for resume
    c.   Title or position of person

Examples for letter: "I have permission to refer. . . .",
"I refer by permission. . . .",
"Mr. Biser has kindly permitted me to
use his name as a reference."

Note: This sentence is followed by mentioning the resume.

Example: On the enclosed resume, you will find additional references and information regarding general qualifications.

5.   Request for an interview — getting action — the clincher!
    a.   Suggest an interview.
    b.   Make that action easy.

Example: "May I have a personal interview at your convenience? I can be reached by telephone at 341-6886."

Or: "May I have a personal interview? If you wish to telephone me, my number is 341-6886."

C.   Things to avoid.

1.   Don't overuse the word "I". Begin every other paragraph with "I". Do not begin more than two consecutive sentences with "I".
2.   Avoid negative statements. If you have no job experience, don't mention it.
3.   Do not begin sentences with words that end in *ing* except "during".
4.   Use connectives for fluidity. Use the dash for emphasis, but sparingly.
5.   Don't mention salary in first contact and, if possible, wait until employer brings up the topic.
6.   Don't copy — be original.

D.   Appraise your letter before you send it.

1.   Appearance
   a.   Stationery — Does it impress favorably?
   b.   Neatness — Is the paper clean?
   c.   Folding — Is it exact and straight?
   d.   Typing — Is it accurate and even?
   e.   Layout — Is it pleasing, balanced, and centered?

2.   Content
   a.   Plan — Is it logical in thought and sequence?
   b.   Paragraphs — Do they indicate thought units?
   c.   Sentences — Are they grammatically correct, varied, and clear?
   d.   Punctuation — Is it correct?
   e.   Spelling — Is it correct?
   f.   Tone — Is it positive?

Resume: While the letter of application should be tailored to fit each employer you send it to, the resume is designed to provide more specific information about your qualifications and background in such a way that it could be sent to any prospective employer. A wide variety of formats are available to present your resume' attractively, but most contain basic information about your career goals, education, experience, extracurricular activities and interests, and a list of references who have given you permission to have prospective employers contact them for information about you. Here is an example of how an attractive resume' might look:

Sarah L. House
1202 Maria Drive
Stevens Point, WI 54481
Telephone: (207)341-4200

CAREER GOAL: To pursue a career in the business field.

EDUCATION: Senior at Stevens Point Area Senior High School, majoring in business education.

WORK EXPERIENCE:

September, 1978 to present   Manager of high school Red and Black Shack school store for class credit. Stevens Point, WI 54481

Close cash register, determine daily sales, order merchandise, pay bills, prepare cash drawer for each day, handle inventory and general store upkeep.

October, 1977 to May, 1978   Part-time clerk high school Red and Black Shack store for class credit. Stevens Point, WI 54481

Operated cash register, made change, sold merchandise, and waited on customers.

June, 1977 to August, 1977   Full-time baby-sitter for Carol Stashek, residence at 762 West River Drive, Stevens Point, WI 54481

Watched one year-old girl, cooked meals, and kept house.

89

EXTRACURRICULAR
ACTIVITIES AND
INTERESTS: Secretary-Treasurer, Orchesis Club
                    St. Stephen's Church Youth Choir
                    Intramural Volleyball
                    Girls' Track Team
                    Sewing, reading, track, music, and camping

REFERENCES: Ms. Judy Jolinski, business education
                    teacher, Stevens Point Area Senior High,
                    1201 North Point Drive, Stevens Point, WI
                    334-5577.

                    Mrs. Alfred Novak, loan teller, Citizens
                    National Bank, 1015 Main Street, Stevens
                    Point, WI 54481, 334-1500, Extension
                    #120.

                    Mrs. Carol Stashek, homemaker, residence
                    702 West River Drive, Stevens Point, WI
                    54481, 341-8751.

Science Reports and Papers. Science reports and technical observations are often organized and footnoted in a manner different from the standard research paper. For example, the paper written to describe a biology or chemistry project or experiment is best understood by the reader if it is organized in the same order as a scientific experiment is carried out:

I. Introduction   A. Provide background information indicating the purpose of the project or experiment. Indicate why you have decided to pursue this topic.

                        B. Establish the hypothesis to be proved by the experiment. Be precise.

                        C. Describe the steps of the experiment necessary to test the hypothesis. Include materials and methods to be used; for example, whether laboratory research, field research, or literature search is to be pursued.

II. Body of Paper D. Record notes or observations on the progress of the experiment as it is carried out and its results.

     1. Include information the reader will need to know to arrive at, or be able to see how you arrive at, your conclusion.

     2. Include pertinent pictures, charts, graphs, or tables to clarify the experiment. All of these illustrations are given the name "figure," are numbered in sequence, and are placed on separate pages at the end of the paper.

Refer to figure within the text of your paper as in this example: ". . . this increase in productivity at 6m can also be seen by the drop in CO_2 (figure 8)."

     3. Include a listing of literature cited comprising all books, pamphlets, magazines, and other sources used in preparing this paper. The sources are listed in alphabetical order by author's last name on a separate page following the conclusion of the paper.

Refer to sources listed in literature cited:
i. When giving a measurement or finding you did not make yourself.
ii. When you wish to give verification to a statement made in your paper.
iii. When quoting a source directly.

Use the following form to "footnote" or refer to literature cited:

". . . the colder the water the greater the amount of O_2 it can contain." (Welch 1962)

III. Conclusion   E.   Draw conclusions based *only* on the data presented.

Note: Avoid the first person point of view ("I") in structuring your paper.

Avoid trick titles for your paper. Be precise, complete, and accurate in designing your title.

Provide a complete table of contents indicating all major areas of the paper including figures.

Follow bibliography form in preparing literature cited. Include exact punctuation. See *Bibliography* for exact form.

In writing the Latin names of plants and animals remember the following:

1.   Family, class, and order are written in the plural and capitalized but *not* underlined.

Cruciferae (mustard family)

   ↓   2.   Genus is written in the singular, capitalized, *and* underlined.

Brassica

   ↓   3.   Species is indicated by genus plus one non-capitalized specific epithet (binomial), *all* underlined.

Brassica oleracea

   ↓   4.   Subspecies (variety) is indicated by genus plus *two* non-capitalized specific epithets (trinomial), *all* underlined.

Brassica oleracea capitata (cabbage)

5.   English versions of Latin names are *not* capitalized or underlined.

Latin   *English*
Arthropoda — arthropod

DATE DUE

SEP 1 0 2001

.5